Cognitive Counseling and Persons with Special Needs

This book is based on my experiences in this field, and no individuals are intended as the basis for the case studies. Steps have been taken to disguise the identities of individuals who may have been used in composites. In short, any resemblance between persons represented here and real persons is coincidental.

Cognitive Counseling and Persons with Special Needs

Adapting Behavioral Approaches to the Social Context

Herbert Lovett

PRAEGER SPECIAL STUDIES • PRAEGER SCIENTIFIC

New York • Philadelphia • Eastbourne, UK
Toronto • Hong Kong • Tokyo • Sydney

Library of Congress Cataloging in Publication Data

Lovett, Herbert.
    Cognitive counseling and persons with special needs.

    Includes index.
    1. Mentally handicapped – Counseling of. 2. Mentally
handicapped – Life skills guides. 3. Adjustment
(Psychology). 4. Cognitive therapy. 5. Behavior
therapy. I. Title.
HV3004.L68 1985   362.2′04256   85-3495
ISBN 0-03-000488-8 (alk. paper)
ISBN 0-03-000487-X (pbk. : alk. paper)

Published in 1985 by Praeger Publishers
CBS Educational and Professional Publishing, a Division of CBS Inc.
521 Fifth Avenue, New York, NY 10175 USA

© 1985 by Praeger Publishers

56789 052 987654321

Printed in the United States of America on acid-free paper

INTERNATIONAL OFFICES

Orders from outside the United States should be sent to the appropriate address listed below. Orders
from areas not listed below should be placed through CBS International Publishing, 383 Madison Ave.,
New York, NY 10175 USA

Australia, New Zealand
Holt Saunders, Pty, Ltd., 9 Waltham St., Artarmon, N.S.W. 2064, Sydney, Australia

Canada
Holt, Rinehart & Winston of Canada, 55 Horner Ave., Toronto, Ontario, Canada M8Z 4X6

Europe, the Middle East, & Africa
Holt Saunders, Ltd., 1 St. Anne's Road, Eastbourne, East Sussex, England BN21 3UN

Japan
Holt Saunders, Ltd., Ichibancho Central Building, 22-1 Ichibancho, 3rd Floor, Chiyodaku, Tokyo, Japan

Hong Kong, Southeast Asia
Holt Saunders Asia, Ltd., 10 Fl, Intercontinental Plaza, 94 Granville Road, Tsim Sha Tsui East,
Kowloon, Hong Kong

**Manuscript submissions should be sent to the Editorial Director, Praeger Publishers, 521 Fifth
Avenue, New York, NY 10175 USA**

Foreword

The most significant manifestation of the tremendous progress made in the field of mental retardation during the past 35 years—ever since the beginning of the revolt of parents protesting the neglect and exclusion for their retarded children—has been the emergence of individuals with mental retardation as persons in their own right, as fellow human beings claiming their place in our society. Attempts to deny this personhood to those who are more severely disabled, still to be found in the literature, prove more nonsensical with every passing year.

Professional judgments of the past such as "totally dependent," "crib case," "vegetable," "untrainable," or "custodial care only," are at the base of the abuse, neglect, and institutionalized cruelty brought to light throughout the country by sworn, unchallenged testimony in numerous class action suits before federal courts. There is no need to dwell on this unfortunate history, but there is indeed urgent need to explore to what extent we can expect services on behalf of persons with severe functional impairment to reflect recognition of their personhood and their right to human dignity and respect.

This volume makes a very substantial contribution toward that end. Written in a lucid and very personal style, as one man's manifesto, or so it appears, it brings to the reader a well-reasoned approach to efforts meeting the needs of this "special" population. Special? Yes, in terms of the varying specific needs such individuals have, but not so special as to be seen as a "class" to be relegated to an inferior status and subjected to deleterious generalizations and exclusionary rules.

Herbert Lovett shows himself in this book as a masterful teacher. His message is clear and convincing: We cannot help others in a meaningful, sustaining way without forming a working relationship with them and, with patience and sensitivity, this can be done also with those profoundly handicapped individuals usually misjudged as unable to communicate.

Even with those who are most severely impaired, he is aiming to find ways of working honestly and respectfully to develop trusting relationships. Throughout one finds cautions about mechanistic uses of behavior techniques. Lovett does not reject Skinner's research and its usefulness; he puts its application in perspective with greater emphasis on the individual person than on specific methodology.

This is a book that deserves wide readership, and its engaging style and practical orientation will appeal to a wide cross section of workers, administrators, volunteers, and advocates in the field.

Gunnar Dybwad
Professor of Human Development
Brandeis University

Acknowledgments

Certain authors, speaking of their works, say, "My book," or "My commentary," "My history," etc. They resemble middle-class people who have a house of their own, and always have "My house" on their tongue. They would do better to say, "Our book," "Our commentary," "Our history," etc., because there is in them usually more of other people's than their own.

Pensées, Pascal

I have been lucky in having a community out of which "our book" has come. Generally, I am grateful to the hundreds of persons I have had the good fortune to know in this service. My life has been enriched by these benefactors not only in the thinking that led to the writing of this book but in the life lived behind it.

Specifically, Jo Allard Krippenstapel helped me put into word and deed what I might have had only as intuition and wish. If she was generous with her ideas and praise, she was also brave in her criticism, and this work would have had more words and less sense without her attention to it.

I had known Drs. Dybwad, Gunnar and Rosemary only by reputation, most specifically through Jo, who has followed their work closely for many years. Although I did not know them personally, their work and personal examples gave shape to the spirit of this book. Since writing it, though, I have had the good fortune at last to meet them and showed them the manuscript. For those thorughout the world who know and love them, the extraordinary generosity of Dr. Dybwad's foreword comes as no surprise. I am profoundly honored by his praise.

Thank you, Tom, Pat, Nancy, John, Jordan; my parents, Herbert and Ruth Lovett; and Michael Dowling, of course.

Contents

— 1 —

Person to Person

My first job as a psychologist included working in an institution for persons who had been labelled severely or profoundly retarded. At meetings we would discuss a problem that someone was presenting, and then we would work out a plan to "control" the problem. Usually, the plan involved a system of rewards or loss of rewards as a consequence for that person's cooperation or lack of it.

At first, I would meet the persons we talked about only accidentally. They never came to the meetings at which they were discussed, and I ran into them only if I went to the ward or perhaps as they were led in a parade of twos from their locked "dormitory" to the cafeteria. Before that time I do not think I had knowingly seen more than three or four persons labelled retarded.

In the meetings I would be presented with the pertinent data around a person's behavior and the direct service workers' understanding of the problem. When I developed a "treatment plan," it was based on my understanding of their perception of what a person I had never met was thinking or doing. Under these conditions I began to feel as if I were not so much a psychologist working with persons as a technician working indirectly with *cases*.

Nothing in my professional training supported my working with such persons in any capacity at all. If anything, I was told to distance myself as much as possible. Some of this was subtly presented (no one in my graduate program wanted to talk about persons labelled retarded, and my entire formal training on the topic consisted of a single lecture). But when I was told, "Don't

1

waste your valuable training on a hopeless situation," that seemed fairly direct.

The way in which my colleagues and supervisors conceptualized the persons I worked with showed how little they understood or cared to understand how such a life is actually lived. One supervisor told me, "It must take a special kind of person to work with those kids." Thinking he genuinely misunderstood my work, I told him, "Actually, I work with adults." "Still," he continued, "it must take a special kind of person to work with those kids." At first, my irritation was that he could not understand that having a disability is not the same as having a perpetual childhood. Later, my anger was that his was the common viewpoint: not only did he need his stereotype, he needed it at the expense of understanding the persons actually involved.

I came to see that labelling persons as "retarded" lumps them together in a dishonest and pointless way. Those we call "retarded" are as much alike as those we call "color blind" or "rich" are alike. We can identify a person as "color blind" as the result of a standardized test. We can label a person "rich" as the result of some arbitrary number connected with financial worth, but we would probably be reluctant to make any more conclusions about a person with one of those labels based on these descriptors alone. When we give a person an IQ test, we are really assessing a relationship between that person and others of the same age who have taken it as well. But when we produce a number and a category of intelligence, there has been the tendency in our culture to make a broader generalization about individuals based on this limited information.

Think of your own IQ, whatever you know or imagine the number to be. If that number were 5 points lower, would you feel differently about yourself? Would you be less "you" or less valuable? Suppose it were 50 or a 100 points lower.

There are almost as many shades of red as there are red objects; each one has a different intensity or saturation of the color. The same might be thought of all the persons who have the IQ of 45 or 145. They share a certain characteristic, but their other characteristics change the meaning of the number. When we talk about "the retarded," we blur the fact that some of these persons have a sense of humor, while others are moody: some are gregarious and talkative, while others are shy and quiet.

The sense of variety and individual difference tends to get washed out by persons who talk about "the retarded." Those persons who are resentful of sentences that begin "All blacks are . . ."

seem not to have much trouble beginning sentences with "The retarded are...." It is not hard for me to hear parallels between the way the persons I work with are talked about and the ways in which other minority groups are still sometimes being described. Unfortunately, the way persons are talked about is often better than they are treated.

As my understanding of "retardation" as a concept became more sophisticated, so, I hope, did my therapeutic approach. I began to see how behaviorism could be used as a political tool that really supported a hierarchy of power between therapists and those they ostensibly served. I began to feel that some of my colleagues were using behaviorism as a way to work *on* others, while I had wanted to work *with* them. I began asking persons to come to meetings where they would be discussed. When I first work with a new group, I am no longer surprised to find the idea resisted: "We won't be able to speak freely with her there." "Why do you insist on this? He really doesn't understand what we are trying to do."

For whatever reason, tradition or worse, the idea of the "staff" as the governing body and those they work for as the governed is one that many persons find comfortable and comforting. The idea of giving this role up is somehow seen as abdication.

When any group makes decisions about a person's life, I am immediately suspicious. Nowhere, outside of the judicial system and the military, can something like this happen. If I thought that this process in some arcane way benefited the person discussed, I would have found it easier to cooperate. Instead, I saw therapy become a power struggle in which those presumed to be in power were consistently losing. The system seemed to rest on the premise that "We know what is best for you, and what's more, we can *make* you *do* what is best." The first part of such a statement could on occasion be true, but the second part is an unethical delusion.

An anecdote will help to illustrate my point. Martha loved coffee. In the time I knew her, she had guzzled coffee boiling from the pot. She had drunk coffee that had been left so long in urns that mold had grown over it. Some had tried to control this by accompanying her everywhere, but regardless of how vigilant they tried to be, she would break away, darting into offices, knocking others over if necessary to get a cup of coffee away from them. Some reacted to this by trying to make coffee even more scarce for her. It got to the point where it was seriously considered banning coffee from all the buildings where Martha either lived or worked.

I could not see how anyone could "win" in this power struggle, although it appeared that everyone involved was prepared to go to great lengths to do so. Martha, for instance, had even been tackled by those intent upon keeping her away from coffee. The plan I proposed would have no "winners" or "losers." It was simply to teach Martha to make coffee, have her buy her own coffee, pot, and cup, and set her up so that whenever she wanted to have a cup she could reach over and pour herself one.

Some persons greeted this innovation by asking, "Why should we give her something for nothing?" From my perspective, Martha had already paid for the coffee and the equipment with her own money. It was not for "nothing." If coffee were the most important thing to this woman, why make it any more important by going to such lengths to keep it from her? Martha had started this program of making her own coffee and governing her own intake when the resentment of those working in direct service grew so great that I thought it unwise to recommend continuing the program. Even more to the point, I had no way of preventing their stopping it.

This also raises the question, "Why should we reward this inappropriate behavior? If she runs into offices, knocking others over for a cup of coffee and we then just give it to her, won't it increase her running into offices?" Certainly, if every person who was knocked over gave Martha a cup of coffee immediately afterward, then she might do more of it, but that was not the plan. The plan was, simply, a person who has coffee next to her will not knock others over for it, unless, of course, her real ambition in life is not to get coffee but instead to be troublesome.

If giving her access to the coffee on her own is seen as "giving in," then what are the alternatives? If we ignore a person racing around and grabbing coffee cups, then we are saying we do not care one way or another. If, at the other extreme, we decide physically to restrain her, then we are teaching her that because we are more powerful she has to yield her wishes to ours. Are these the lessons we really want to teach? Martha in fact had already learned that being stronger was an asset and, indeed, some persons complained that she had started forcing others to "share" their coffee with her. The did not see how they themselves were the models for this.

Rather than labelling the way a person acts as "inappropriate" and then giving ourselves license to demand she change it, we could try another interpretation and another approach: we could guess that Martha acts this way because she has learned poor social strategies. By "making concessions," and giving her a new so-cial milieu in which to learn new social strategies, Martha could work with us on a solution to the problem by cooperating rather than our coercing her to change because she inconveniences us.

This raises the question of who is better able to make "conces-sions" or adjustments in routine: those providing the service or those served? I do not know how coffee came to be so important for Martha, but at other times it had been used as a reinforcement for her in a "behavioral program" to get her to stay in the class-room. Once her demand for it exceeded their willingness to provide it for her, though, they tried to reinforce her for not trying to get coffee.

This pointed out, for me, a shortcoming of this typical ap-proach. Once a person has defined a point of conflict, in this case, coffee, the ideal would be to move the struggle to a neutral area so that everyone could work together without conflict. In this situa-tion, for example, rather than struggle with Martha over coffee, cof-fee could have been made neutral by being readily available to her. Instead, the persons working with Martha had accepted her defi-nition of coffee as important, and they focused on it as she did, as if it were the ordinary preoccupation of all persons.

My interest in suggesting the intervention of "giving in" was to let Martha know that coffee was valuable to her; so naturally she should have access to it. But because it was not so valuable as to necessitate being guarded, she should determine when and how much she would drink. This approach gave her responsibility for setting limits as she needed them to be set, with the implicit un-derstanding that she was the person best suited to know what those limits should be.

Behavioral approaches often have a different context for the persons we work with than for most other persons in other situa-tions. For example, I might want to quit smoking. I go to a be-havioral therapist who works out with me the conditions under which I like smoking and a system that helps make not smoking preferable for me. If I can go a day without cigarettes, I get to re-ward myself with an extra good dinner. If I can go a week, I get to see a movie. If I can go a year, then I can take a trip I have wanted to go on and can now more easily afford with the money I have saved from not buying cigarettes. Obviously, this is a highly sim-plified example, but the point is that the therapist and I have worked out the program together. If the therapist did not have my cooperation in doing so, then she would have had to guess what would appeal to me enough to be reinforcing. If she had guessed that I would consider a football game worth a week of nonsmoking, she would have developed a less effective program for me if my real passion is Italian opera.

Another important aspect to this example is that I have decided not only to stop smoking but have also chosen the therapist to help me do it. The program will have virtually no chance of success if a group of friends, relatives, consulting professionals, and well-meaning passersby decide that it is time for me to quit. Similarly, even if I myself decide it is time to stop, the program will have less of a chance of success if someone tells me I must work with this therapist and none other. Under these conditions, I could be lucky and be assigned someone congenial, but it is more likely that I will enjoy working with someone whom I feel I can accept or decline than with someone whom I have been assigned to. Finally—some behaviorists have difficulty in explaining and understanding this—I will probably have a better experience learning to quit successfully if in some intangible way I like and trust the therapist and have some faith in her abilities to help me with this problem.

So, when a consultant sits down to devise a "treatment plan" for a person who is not even present, how well do you think the plan is going to work? Having to work this way—without the person's being present—I have had to guess. By asking, "If I were this person, what would this situation mean to me? How could acting this way make sense for me?" I have tried to begin seeing the way persons act as their best attempt at adaptation. One person lost patience with this and scolded me: "You've got to stop thinking like that. They're retarded and you're not. It's completely different." My point, of course, is that it is not.

Even when we are dealing with a very simple problem, I do not think it has the same impact for persons to have a decision thrust upon them as it does for them to make the decision, regardless of how well intentioned we might be. I have worked with persons "much too retarded to know any better" who were able to help me in a substantial way to work out a program for themselves. But even small points can make the difference between a good program and one that is relatively ineffective. For example, a group working on its own might say, "If Lou can go an entire week without 'tantrumming,' we'll take her to MacDonald's." But when we ask Lou (after explaining precisely what we mean by "tantrumming"), she might say that she would prefer to go shopping for clothes. The effort required is no different, but for Lou, our approach might mean more since she had chosen it herself rather than having had something similar assigned to her.

The model that behavior modification has used is that if we can break behaviors into small enough units then we can change the way a person acts. This approach has been the only way some persons have been able to learn complicated tasks they might otherwise never have been able to do. This approach has allowed persons labelled retarded to do vocational tasks that compare competitively with other persons in the work force.

But I am not altogether sure this is the way we want to teach social skills. The systems of cues and reponses for social functioning are not so easily kept consistent the way vocational tasks can be. Instead, the premise of the treatment approaches described here is that behavior is dependent upon social environment and that manipulating the social environment will most effectively manipulate the way a person acts. The best place for a person to learn a skill is in the natural environment that skill is used. So if we are to teach normal social skills, we should be prepared to do so in places that are in fact socially normal. We have forgotten, sometimes, that there is an interaction between the person and the environment, that each acts in turn on the other: first, the institution is created for persons with developmental disability; then it begins to create persons with developmental disability.

Some of the basic premises of behaviorism do not seem difficult to grasp. These simple principles have often been demonstrated as effective; so there is a strong temptation for those who feel they need to "control" the problem another person presents to use behavioral strategies. Behavioral principles "work" without having to explain them to the person they are being used upon; indeed, some behaviorists argue against informing the person of how the plan works since this is unnecessary for its success. I have seen technically well-considered plans fail because they did not take into account the personal wishes and needs of the person the plan was designed for. This sort of off-the-rack behaviorism is exactly what psychology as a science and behaviorism as a practice do not need.

From a practical, day-to-day standpoint, there is probably no one who has done more to influence the treatment of typically institutionalized persons than B. F. Skinner. In spite of the controversy that has surrounded his work at the theoretical level, his contribution at the clinical level is indisputable. Where traditional therapies would not or could not be effective, behaviorism has been. Those who were once labelled and dismissed as "untrainable" have been able to present themselves with behavioral training not only as "trainable" but even as skilled.

Perhaps it was in reaction to the psychoanalytic emphasis on insight that made behaviorism come to look at the mind as a "black box." Rather than delve into the early origins and symbols of a behavior, behaviorists have been interested only in changing it. They have been, historically, more interested in finding out where a behavior is going than where it has come from.

My first experience, as I have mentioned, was with persons living on a locked ward in an institution. Those who lived there were considered so handicapped that they lived under constant supervision. In some ways, my first "treatment plan" was also my most instructive one.

Stewart was given to scratching others. This was painful, of course, to the persons scratched, but it also isolated Stewart from ordinary social relationships since almost everyone who could avoid him did. As a result, those who worked with him felt it important to find a way to change the way he acted. Specifically, they wanted a "behavioral treatment plan." Stewart had been assessed as "severely retarded"; so I was advised to choose a concrete reinforcer in working with him. Since he liked raisins, it was agreed that he be given a few raisins every 15 minutes through his waking hours when he had not scratched or bitten. I thought the real reinforcer would be the attention others would be giving when they approached him and said, "You've had a good quarter hour, Stewart, here are some raisins that you've earned." If, on the other hand, Stewart did bite or scratch someone, then he would not get the raisins that quarter hour, and this reinforcement would be given, along with sympathy, to the victim. In this way, I hoped, Stewart would think: "By not scratching, I get others to give me attention and a snack. Scratching deprives me of valuable things."

This "plan" worked with almost textbook perfection. After the first few days, Stewart began to scratch at a much higher rate, but this quickly dropped off so that he was scratching at a rate well below baseline. I say with "almost textbook perfection" since there were effects I had not expected.

Around seven o'clock one evening, I dropped by the ward to see how the program was working. All of the data collection sheets for that shift had been filled out for each quarter hour until shift change at *eleven* with the notation, "Good—given reward."

This meant that either the program had done its job and the persons working with it were through or that it had inadvertently made them clairvoyant. I decided that what this really meant was that, despite my most supportive attention to the demands this program made on their time, they had been unwilling to tell me that giving the reinforcement every 15 minutes had gone from being effective to being, for them, a nuisance.

My first lesson, then, was that no program is complete that does not pay attention to the needs of those doing it at least as efficiently as it does to the needs of the identified person.

My second lesson was that "fixing" a single "behavior" could upset the ecology of a person's life by changing the entire system in which he lived. Specifically, I had not counted on training 30 "severely retarded" persons how to feign having been scratched in order to get a handful of raisins.

—2—

Behaviorism in a Social Context

Psychology has had the same challenges to being "scientific" that medicine has had. One of the ways it has met that challenge has been through behaviorism. In order to study behavior scientifically, behavioral psychologists broke complex actions into small and observable units. This was necessary in order to understand the principles underlying "behavior." But ordinary life is more complex than the life behaviorism studied in its early stages. For those of us working with persons labelled retarded, there is a dilemma: how do we provide opportunities for a "normal" life and use the knowledge behaviorism has shown valid through research? The challenge is to provide an environment for the persons we work for in which they can benefit both from behavioral research and the expectations of ordinary life.

One analogy to this is the way that medicine first developed as a "scientific art." In the last century the physician was in a similar position that the psychologist is in today: the field was seen as a healing art that could, on occasion, be demonstrated. But it was generally seen as too unreliable in its performance to be seen as a real science. Furthermore, the physician was competing with a number of home remedies and over-the-counter nostrums that had as much validity for the public as the physician's own interventions.

One of the ways that medicine was able to make advances in the reliability of its practice and in its public esteem was that it started to study pathology in the microcosm. To become more of a science, medicine dispensed with the moral interpretation of ill-

11

ness and looked in a strictly mechanistic way at illnesses, focusing on single treatments as they applied to isolated diseases. In this way, medical science was able to validate statistically that one therapy worked better than another.

But orthodox medicine, by focusing so strictly on a narrow view of the patient, often left sick persons with the feeling that they were not being treated as individuals so much as "the gall bladder in 5-2-C." Even beyond this was the larger concern shared by physicians themselves: can we really treat people's illnesses as if their maladies existed independently of the rest of their lives? Can we really not look at lifestyle as contributing as much to an individual's health as anything else? The answer to these questions seems to have been no. Today, for a number of reasons, some of them philosophical, others financial (they are not, of course, mutually exclusive), there is a much greater concern on the part of the health community to point out habits that hurt rather than help. The general public is more aware of the benefits of exercising and eating moderately. This attitude on the part of health professionals and the public at large does not mean that research medicine is in low repute. It means that the findings of research medicine are more rapidly adapted into ordinary, daily living.

Similarly, my interest is not to disregard what behavioral research has found. Behaviorism has made gains in its understanding by breaking complicated behavior into small, observable units. Rather than isolate a specific behavior and treat it in isolation, I am interested in seeing how that behavior serves the person's sense of adaptation to his or her environment. So while looking at a specific problem is a first consideration, I try never to make it the final one.

* * *

One issue in using behavioral strategies is attention. We almost always assume that attention is a highly positive intervention. When we withhold attention, the person we are ignoring is supposed to feel the loss and shape his or her behavior more closely to our expectations. This makes good, common sense but occasionally poor practice. For example, if someone is doing something to get our attention—think of something obnoxious—our tendency is to ignore it and show the person that we do not bestow our attentions without a price. My experience is that what happens next is an increase in the obnoxious behavior. This increase might be part of a learning curve, but in reality obnoxious behavior can easily escalate to the point where it can no longer be easily ignored. In fact, if doing something we consider obnoxious is a person's main, or only, way to communicate, then increasing it is a logical reaction.

For example, suppose you wish to speak to your "significant other" at breakfast. You might mumble, "please pass the marmalade." Your S.O. ignores you. You think to yourself, "I have mumbled. I will speak more distinctly." But when you do, you are again ignored. You are confused and perhaps a little irritated. You speak with greater voice, only to be ignored again. I think as soon as you decide that this person is not deaf and is ignoring you on purpose for some unexplained reason, that is the point at which you become angry.

My experience has been that persons labelled retarded are rarely present when "behavioral plans" are decided upon and worked out. As a result, they are suddenly put into situations where others are acting differently toward them for no apparent reason. Suppose your significant other had become vexed with your requests for marmalade and had decided that ignoring you was the best method to get you to stop. "Behavioral plans" often use this as a strategy. Of course, it would be simpler, less condescending, and far more cheerful to say, "When you ask for marmalade at breakfast, I get irritated." Without being told that this was why you were being ignored, your response might be anything from angry confusion to angry divorce.

I am presuming that you have some relatively sophisticated way of communicating, either through speaking or signing. But suppose you were, as many of the persons I work with are, unable to communicate easily what you feel and think. And suppose that as you became angrier and angrier you were treated not with sympathy or understanding but with plans that ignored your anger. Under these conditions, many of us would soon become "out of control" with rage or eventually seriously depressed. But if you were called "retarded," your depression might well be seen as compliance and the program that got you there a great success.

Trying to understand persons who communicate with difficulty can make us uncomfortable. When a person who cannot ask verbally for something tugs at my sleeve, I try to find out what he wants. If it is not obvious, I ask. Some just want to say "Hi!" and tugging on a sleeve is how they do it. Even though this is not the usual way of doing it, I do not ignore it. If I am going to be with a person for a while, though, I would start to change this way of saying "Hi" to something more traditional (such as waving). But if I ignore the tug on the sleeve, I run the risk of inadvertently saying, "I didn't notice you." If I keep ignoring his efforts, he can become increasingly aggressive to the point where ignoring him is painful if not dangerous.

This is not to suggest that ignoring a person is always wrong, only that it needs to be made clear to the person why we are doing it and what alternatives he can use to engage us once again.

If a person is not able to tell us specifically what it is she wants, we have to use guesswork. Usually, when a person does any sort of acting out I take it to mean, if there is no other clue, that she wants to do something different from what she has been given to do. When a person whines, throws work, or hits the person next to her, I interpret it to mean "Give me something else to do." Often, when a person throws work, I will say, "It looks like you need to take a break." To me this simply states the obvious: a person who wants to be working will not be flinging the work materials about. Furthermore, it is covertly saying, "We are here to help. Let's establish a relationship that reflects that fact."

I have been criticized more than once that this approach is unrealistic because if persons "misbehave" they should at least lose a reward and perhaps even have to make up the loss. The argument used against this approach takes a predictable course. "People need limits set on them. They need to know we are in charge. They need to pay the consequences of their behavior. If I were to throw work around, I would have to pay for the damage, and I would also be docked the salary I could have earned or even get fired." I understand this attitude and sympathize with the sense of inadequacy it represents. But why should we ask persons to assume the negative side of normal responsibilities when they have not been given the opportunity to enjoy the rewards of such responsibilities? And why do we take a group we have defined by their limitations and set stricter limits on them?

Those who seem so eager to punish what they do not approve of do not seem to be so concerned about guaranteeing certain basic rights. For instance, are the persons they want to punish earning minimum wage? Few persons I work with in workshops earn more than $10 in a 35-hour week. So if persons working in direct service are given harsher consequences for "misbehavior," it is also true that they are being given greater compensation for acting appropriately.

I think identifying with the persons we work with is a helpful starting point in considering the challenges they present us. A helpful question to ask is, "How would I feel in that position?" Certainly, the answer is not always useful since what might bother me would be a pleasure for you, but it is important as a way of keeping the person we are working for in mind. My experience is that some persons are willing to make this comparison between themselves and others only when they are justifying punishment. If we are serious about helping others to live normal lives, I think we should be prepared to extend to them special benefits first and then the responsibilities that go with those benefits. As it stands now, we perversely make those persons with disabilities work harder to earn less.

* * *

At this point, I would like to give an example of what I mean and to show how this differs from the more traditional therapy given to persons labelled retarded.

Gregory was a man with Down's Syndrome who lived with his parents and attended a training program in basic skills. He had been assessed as too severely impaired for formalized IQ testing, but an assessment using the Vineland Scale of Social Maturity gave him a social age of 2.9 years. This placed him in the profound range of social adaptation. His program consisted of simple sorting tasks, puzzles, some assembly work, and occasional shopping trips.

While working Gregory would make noises to himself that after a few minutes became a whine. When this was ignored, his whining developed into crying. If he were still ignored, he would become visibly upset and throw his work around the room. A previous psychological evaluation had made the recommendation of "a total ignoring program to decrease throwing behavior." This was unsuccessful because it is difficult—and usually absurd—to ignore a person throwing things in a crowded room. This became an especially poor strategy when Gregory threw a protective helmet that one of the other trainees wore—while the trainee was wearing it. In other programs this behavior had been typically addressed with his losing a privilege at break time or in being "timed out."

"Time out" means different things in different places. Sometimes work is taken away until a person is thought to be back in control. It can mean making a person sit in a chair that faces a corner of the room. "Time out" sometimes means being "escorted" to a room, usually with no furniture, and being held down on the floor or kept there until someone decides the person is "back in control." I am told there are persons who find "time out" the only way to control themselves. I am not surprised to hear this. Few programs teach socially acceptable ways of being angry or even respect the basic right (and inevitable need) to feel anger. And if the persons in direct service do not know acceptable ways of getting angry, I do not expect the persons directly served by them will.

The behavioral rationale for "time out" is that the person "misbehaves" for attention. If we can remove the rewarding attention, then the "misbehavior" will stop. Since some persons do act unpleasantly just to generate excitement, I understand how ignoring them could help them to stop. But one "behavior" can be used to satisfy more than one motive. To assume that episodes of "acting out" will be diminished by "timing out" is probably correct. Punishment can be effective in diminishing a person's interest in doing something. The problem is that punishment tends to suppress *all* interest in doing things.* When others, especially those who cannot communicate easily with me, act unpleasantly or unpredictably, my best response is not to punish them for expressing themselves. It makes more sense to ask, "What are you trying to tell me when you do that?"

When Gregory began to make whining noises, his teacher would say to him, "You seem upset. Why don't you take a break?" Since he seemed to enjoy lying on a mat, he would be offered one to lie on. We thought he would benefit more from this if he saw this as a real attempt to help him regain control. By giving him ways to tense and relax himself, we thought he might feel more at ease than if he were left to lie on the mat passively. He was encouraged to try some gross motor activity such as lifting his arms above him as he lay on his back, followed by a rest break. After a few minutes of this, he was given the opportunity to go back to work. If he needed more time on the mat, he would get it; if not, he could try working again. The important element of this was to give Gregory what he wanted, as best we could understand his wishes and as best we could provide for him. This way he did not have to throw his work around the room to get attention or anything else.

---

*Another problem with "time out" is that while it punishes the person being timed out it is negatively reinforcing for the person doing the timing out. By having a troublesome person removed, the person doing the "time out" is rewarded. The net effect of this is that this procedure is more likely to be repeated since it has such potential to be reinforcing. At the same time the person being "timed out" is less likely to want to do anything at all. My experience is that this procedure is a wedge that pushes persons into opposite directions. Some are feeling relieved at the same time another person is feeling oppressed.

His teacher was concerned about some possible problems with this approach. What should she do, for instance, if he refused to get on the mat? The answer came from asking, "What are we trying to accomplish here?" We were trying to give Gregory the message, "We are concerned with your feelings. If you feel upset, let us help." If we were serious about this message, then we would take our cues about what to do from Gregory himself. So if he refused to lie on the mat, we would then offer him the chance just to sit; or, if he needed it, to walk around. His teacher would remove the work he was doing from his immediate area and say, "If you don't feel like lying on the mat, then maybe just taking a break here will be helpful." Again, after a few minutes, he was to be given the opportunity to resume work.

If, by chance, his teacher did not read Gregory's cues accurately or—as was often the case, he gave no cues at all—and he actually threw work, then another trainee was to be asked to help the teacher pick the work up.*

There was also some concern that he might choose to get onto the mat but would then kick at persons passing by or bang on the wall. If this happened, he was to be told, "You still seem upset, and if you think banging will help let us help you. Here is a pillow to bang so you won't hurt your hand. You can't hurt the pillow. Go ahead and bang away." This was a less satisfying solution because it is less acceptable in ordinary social situations. We wanted to persuade Gregory that he could be both angry and socially acceptable at the same time. So we decided to attach a slight cost to this less satisfactory choice. If he started to bang, he would be asked to keep banging past the point at which he wanted to stop. If he banged the pillow ten times, he would be asked to bang it three more. Doing this would make banging a pillow slightly less appealing than the strategy we were trying to teach. My interest in this was to give Gregory ways of getting irritated without looking foolish. Generally speaking, a person banging a pillow looks more foolish than a person taking a break from a stressful situation.

Using this approach, what would be the best way to respond when Gregory hit another trainee? His teacher thought these as-

---

*The trainee who helped pick up the work actually volunteered to do so and seemed pleased to be helpful. The message we were trying to give Gregory here was, "When you are appropriate in letting us know you need a break, we are happy to help you by cooperating; but, when you act without regard for others, we will try to help them feel better instead." In this way, we were presenting Gregory with a socially normal choice to make.

saults were motivated by Gregory's need to get "attention." If he felt ignored, he would hit another trainee. This was too serious to be ignored, and yet she did not want to be unnecessarily punitive. Even here, though, it was possible to address this effectively without punishment. When he hit another trainee, he was to be given the same set of options that he would have had he thrown work. He would be told, "You seem upset. Why don't you take a break?" If he wanted to, he could get onto the mat. Or he could take a break at his work station by just sitting there while work was cleared away from him. This was to be done quickly with a minimum of eye contact. Then the person who had been hit was to be given reassurance. Gregory's hitting was more irritating than harmful; so the person he had hit needed TLC more than first aid. The training area was small so Gregory got to see the person he had frightened getting the attention and concern he could have been getting himself.

Gregory had other ways of engaging attention, such as taking his clothes off. His previous instructors had not wanted him to be seen doing this as it reflected badly on them as much as on Gregory himself. Gregory had found this an effective way of engaging others on his own terms. One underlying assumption I try to make in drawing up ways to work is that it is much better for everyone to learn to cooperate than it is to try to compete. Just as I do not care to coerce any person into doing anything that that person objects to, I also do not care to feel coerced by others.

So Gregory's approach would be met with a failure on our part to cooperate in the expected manner. If he took off his shoes, his teacher would take them and say, "You seem to need to take your shoes off. I'll put them over here for you." This would make it clear to him that if he needed to take off any garment, the person around him would not intervene except to store the clothing nearby. When he wanted his shoes back, though, his teacher was to emphasize to him how much he was responsible for his actions by saying, "Since you needed to take your shoes off, let's not hurry to put them back on again. Let's make sure that having them off has done all the good it can for you." The quotations used here are intended simply to convey the spirit of the conversation. His teacher used whatever language she felt comfortable with to express these ideas and attitudes. It is difficult to convey the tone of voice used here. The purpose was not to teach Gregory *consequences* so much as ordinary, dignified social responsibility. This was not a subtle game of showing him who was boss but simply a way of underscoring that his decisions would be respected.

It is reasonable to ask what the difference is between saying "You need a break" and giving him an option of how to spend time away from work and using the traditional "time-out" approach. From the behavioral point of view, there is perhaps no difference. In both cases, he is separated from his work. But there is an entirely different implication between these approaches. When we enforce a "time-out" procedure, we are taking work away or forcibly moving the person away. When we use this alternative approach, we are offering a choice and giving the person something.

I do not at all see this as simply playing with words. I think the different ways of describing these procedures reflect a difference in basic attitude. Suppose you decide, for reasons convenient to yourself, to take a vacation starting next Wednesday at noon. You would not feel at all the same about this if instead you were told to take it starting next Wednesday. One situation is the result of your own choices; the other is something you are forced to accept. In each case you are getting the time off, but I would expect you to react to these situations quite differently. Is it just playing with words then to describe these behaviorally similar situations so differently?

If Gregory chose the mat when it was first offered, then calmed himself and returned to work, he was to be given informal praise by his teacher in the form of "You must be proud of yourself for having chosen...." One way of thinking of this is that Gregory is being reinforced for appropriate behavior. Of course he is, but the point of this was to encourage him to make decisions and to experience having those decisions respected. If this had been a polite way of getting Gregory to work on our terms, I suspect Gregory would have sensed this and found a way of testing our goodwill. The "behavior" we wanted to encourage was the sense that he himself was responsible for his actions and that he was the one who would feel best or worst about his choices.

Sometimes, when others are cooperative or do something well, we say, "I am so proud of you for having...." as if our approval were a great reward. Of course, it might be, but what are we going to say when the person does badly? "I am so humiliated that you...."? Or what if the person wants to inflict despair? The message we want to convey is: "Your choices affect you more than anyone; so make them according to your needs." And we want to say this in a supportive way. The situation is not greatly improved if all we are saying is, "Swim or drown; it's your life."

During the brief baseline period we used, Gregory had had eight episodes of throwing work in the five days of program. These increased almost immediately to eight episodes in the first two days since this program was begun. But over an eight-week period, this style of responding had diminished to virtually nothing (one incident in two weeks).

His teacher noted other changes in him beyond the ones anticipated by this program. For instance, after a couple of weeks, Gregory started leaving his work area and quietly getting the mat out for himself to relax on. Apparently, he felt he had the authority to take care of his frustration on his own, and he started to do so in an appropriate manner. Or if he needed assistance in getting the mat, he would signal for someone to help him. When he did throw his work, he appeared to be irritated to see Carolyn, another trainee, get the teacher's attention while she helped pick up. Gregory responded to this by taking his shoes off and throwing them at Carolyn. Incidentally, Carolyn used an adaptive foam wedge to help her sit more comfortably in a straight back chair. After she had established herself as the person who got status for helping to pick up Gregory's work, Gregory, interestingly enough, started imitating her by using foam wedges for his chair.

Gregory's teacher met with his parents to review the progress he had made and was persuasive in getting them to give Gregory more responsibility at home. Gregory's mother had long thought of him as a permanent child. Because of this, she felt she was doing the best she could for him by letting him spend weekends alone in his room playing with puzzles. But with the teacher's encouragement, she began to think of ways that Gregory could help around the house. To his mother's surprise, Gregory was able to vacuum, set the table, help in preparing food for meals, as well as help in working around the yard. So the progress that he was making in his day program was generalizing to greater competence— and status—at home. A situation like this can begin to become as self-perpetuating as a bad one: as Gregory showed he could do things his parents had thought impossible, they became more inclined to give him more challenging things to do.

* * *

Rather than focusing on a specific "problem behavior," the approach I have suggested uses the way persons act as the best clue of how they feel they have been treated. Rather than impose a program that will eliminate or even decrease the presenting problem, it changes the world in which the "problem" has appeared. Once the environment has properly changed, this maladaptive strategy becomes unnecessary. One assumes that persons respond to a situation with the best answer they have. If the answer is a "problem," it is usually a problem for others as well. We are most responsible for providing the environment for a person to demonstrate success and not continued failure.

The change in Gregory's training program gave him an opportunity to change the way he responded to it. After a while, when Gregory was able to express his frustration with his work reasonably, his teacher began asking why he was still expressing frustration at all. We decided that what was at fault was the work he was asked to do. Was there a way to make his work more valuable to him by presenting him with greater variety and challenge? There was a limit to the variety of work his teacher could provide for Gregory.* To increase his sense of involvement, though, she decided to let him choose his own work. There are those who object to this on the grounds that "these people" will keep choosing the same thing day after day and never learn anything new. But my concern is that by doing only what we tell them, they are learning something far more harmful: that *we* make their choices for them. I think it is better for a person to learn that the persons he works with are there more to help than to enforce. Even if trainees chose the same thing all the time, they could be invited to try something else to help them learn new skills. But there is a world of difference between choosing something to do and being told to do it.

Gregory's teacher found work used in a vocational training program for him to try. Some other teachers thought the tasks too "advanced" for Gregory to understand. Once he saw what the work required, however, he did it with concentration. He apparently enjoyed not only the challenge of the new work but also the opportunity to choose it from his usual, routine tasks. And he did

---

*The limit on the work available to Gregory was not because his teacher felt that he could do so much and no more. There was a limit to the materials available to his teacher to use. One of the problems with "vocational training" programs is the seriously limited number of skills they attempt to teach. In virtually every "vocational" program I have worked with or visited, the workers are packaging or sorting. The sorts of jobs these skills lead to, coincidentally enough, seem more often to be found in sheltered workshops than in competitive job placements. The primary problem with "vocational training" programs is that they almost always lead to more "training" and almost never to a "vocation."

not need to cry or even to take breaks on the mat using this approach.

It appeared that the noise of the cafeteria bothered him; so Gregory ate his lunch quickly and then spent the rest of his free time back in the quiet classroom. His teacher encouraged him to go through the work materials so that he could set up his own assignments for the afternoon. Gregory and his teacher made an agreement that whatever he chose himself he would actually do. None of us was surprised to find that he was able to plan his own work for the rest of the day with minimal supervision. The important accomplishment was for him to see that he could make his own decisions and negotiate the consequences. This approach was structured so as to be more positive than negative: he himself decided what he would do.

I would emphasize here that Gregory is not the sort of person who would ordinarily inspire confidence in others. His level of assessed functioning was far lower than his demonstrated abilities. A person labelled "profoundly retarded" would not typically be expected to understand and make the kinds of decisions that Gregory did in this program. But that is precisely the point I want to make: that our perceptions and assessments of a person's abilities can become self-fulfilling prophecies. When we assume that individuals can learn to do anything, regardless of the label or presumed disability, then we are leaving it up to them to tell us their limits. For years we have defined the ceiling of capability for an entire population of our fellow citizens by saying "They will be able to do this much and no more." And when we do not give them the opportunity to do more, the prophecy always comes true. Only when the lives of all allow the maximum opportunity for development will we know what an individual can really do.

—3—

Behavior Modification

An axiom used in therapy is that one's long suit is also one's short suit. Some persons work so hard to be organized that it prevents them from paying attention to their lives. The composer John Cage tells the story of giving a lecture where he suggested that the students not take notes but just listen instead. One student kept writing and when he asked her about it, she looked back in her notebook and saw she had indeed written: "Don't take notes."

I think something like this has happened in our work with persons labelled retarded. Sometimes we have become so caught up with "behavior" that we forget to listen to what that behavior is telling us. Sometimes when we are confused by the challenges a person presents to us, behavior analysis provides an opportunity to get away from the situation and look at it more objectively. But once we have developed a way to work with a person, we are then working not with data but with an individual. Behavioral research has made psychology a more empirical science, but it has not concentrated on developing a social context for its use. Because of that, the techniques to change behavior have been used as part of "treatment" rather than of training for persons labelled retarded.

Typically, persons labelled retarded have better vocational skills than social ones. But this is because we spend more time in providing training opportunities than we do in providing social opportunities. Instead of using behavioral analysis to teach vocational skills, we use behavior modification to enforce social norms. It is important to point out that this has less to do with behavior modification than it does with those who use it. Using an empirical, data-based model for working with others often allows—even forces—us to forget them and to focus our attention instead on their "behavior." This is a useful tool if we are trying to teach a person how to repair a radio, but it seems an odd approach if we are trying to help someone learn how to socialize at mealtimes.

The emphasis on data can result in our continued maintenance of a psychological distance from others. If we do this, we can sacrifice a sense of equality and mutual respect we might have had. It is easier to feel awe or condescension, pity or fear, when we also feel we have little in common with someone anyway. Without a sense of equality and mutual respect, it is much harder to work cooperatively with someone. By "working cooperatively with someone" I mean considering other persons' preferences, "style," "personality"—in other words *them*. Objective analysis is a useful first—but a poor only—step in meeting behavioral challenges. Successful intervention requires much more than just "treating" a single behavior.

In working with persons labelled retarded, we see today two apparently conflicting trends. On the one hand, there is the general consensus that it is legally, ethically, and emotionally wrong to deprive others of an ordinary life for reasons of their assessed intellectual functioning. On the other hand, the most common "treatment" made available to such persons has been technical rather than personal. This presents us with a challenge: how to make what behavioral science has learned under experimental conditions available in ordinary environments. It is not that the *principles* of behavioral research are at issue; their applications are.

For example, reinforcers can help in teaching a complicated task if we break it into small, more easily acquired steps. Reinforcing each step as it is learned leads a person (or an animal) relatively painlessly to mastery. Skinner, for example, has championed the use of programmed instruction that breaks large concepts into small steps, moving from the familiar to the new. This allows students to learn at their own pace. Used in this way, behavioral principles have been used to help persons learn what they might otherwise never have even been taught.

Behavioral principles seem easy to understand, and this sets them up to be the easy solutions to the more complex behavioral challenges. The apparent simplicity of these principles makes them more available to persons who do not completely understand them or those they use them on. This promotes bad treatment under the guise of "science" and helps keep persons with challenges away from us, by allowing us to armor ourselves with counters, stopwatches and clipboards rather than working more openly and directly.

The reason for this, I think, is historical: behaviorism's earliest subjects were laboratory animals (especially pigeons) as they were observed in experiments using a Skinner Box.* This is an example of behaviorism's strength being simultaneously a weakness: on the one hand, these experiments showed that animals previously thought to be less trainable—hence less intelligent—than others could learn complicated tasks and that these same principles of task analysis could be used to help persons with cognitive handicaps as well. On the other hand, since this model used animals that were observed as animals, the model did not establish a social context for these principles to be applied in.

The Skinner Box is simple enough: it has a magazine that stores food pellets, a light that can serve as a stimulus, a button to be pecked or a lever to be pressed, and an electrified metal grid that can be used to shock the animal. The box is made of plexiglass to keep out extraneous and undesired environmental variables as much as possible. This device is quite ingenious if we want to study only one specific behavior. As a laboratory tool, it is like the Petri dish or the agar plate, which allows us to study microorganisms in isolation rather than as they occur in life.

If, when an animal presses the bar, a pellet of food drops into the cage, the animal gradually learns that pressing the bar produces food pellets. The behaviorist can define food pellets then as "reinforcing." If, instead of food pellet, the animal is given an electric shock, it will then learn not to press the bar. Because it

---

*Skinner (1983) himself prefers that it not be called this. Unfortunately, there is no alternative name by which this device is so readily recognized.

leads to a decrease in behavior, the shock would be considered "punishing."*

The behavioral approach has not speculated on how the animal or a person "understands" this information. Such speculation, because it cannot be validated, is considered working with "hypothetical constructs" (which Skinner calls "explanatory fictions"). Behaviorism considers the brain or the psyche as a "black box": information goes in, something unknown and perhaps unknowable happens, and "behavior" comes out.

I do not mean to imply that behaviorism is less a science for not formulating hypotheses to explain the organism's internal process. That would be like criticizing a musician for not knowing where the composer got the music. This insistence that "nonbehavioral" processes are not within the realm of behaviorism gives it a more "empirical" credibility. But these ideas do not immediately provide a natural social context in which to use them.

One of the confusions that is caused by this is the different applications that behavioral principles can have. Breaking a situation into small, observable units can be used, for example, in both train-

---

*Here is an example that has misled some who try to use these ideas on persons labelled retarded: since we assume the rat "likes" to eat, food should be reinforcing. But there are any number of environmental factors that can influence this. A common error in "behavioral treatment" for persons labelled retarded is to assume that if something pleasant is offered as a reward it should be reinforcing. Something rewarding *might* be reinforcing, but we have to validate its value as a reinforcement by seeing if it actually does cause an increase in the targeted behavior. It is often assumed that persons who are labelled "profoundly" or "severely" retarded need primary reinforcers. My own experience is quite otherwise. Persons who have been labelled in this way are as much alike as persons with any other label are alike. Automatically using a food reinforcer for such persons shows that we have underestimated their sensibilities; or, it shows that we have resorted to food because there is nothing else around. In both of these cases, the reason for the food reinforcer rests on our perception and treatment of the person and not with the person we are supposedly serving. We often do not apply our "strict" principles to ourselves half so stringently as we do on those we attempt to help. That is to say, if we took seriously what we believe to be true, then we would check our plans out with the persons our plans intend to help and learn from *them* what they would consider reinforcing *and* check to see if the introduction of that "reinforcement" actually increased the target behavior. Regardless of how pleasant and desirable we might find a "reinforcement," it cannot really be called that without a *demonstrable* increase of the behavior.

ing and in therapy. How we apply these principles to persons who have been labelled "retarded" reflects how we understand them. If we see their retardation as a handicap that is eased with special training, then we will use behavioral principles in one way (i.e., task analysis). But if we see a person's retardation as requiring "treatment," then we will use these same principles to quite another purpose (i.e., behavior modification).

Using behavioral principles to "treat" a person's retardation seems the least defensible application, and yet it is the one most commonly used. This application makes a series of clinical and political judgments that begin and end erroneously: that retardation in and of itself is somehow a "pathology" that requires "treatment," often in the form of "behavior management," as if we were discussing the control of a virulent agent of contagion.

Retardation is not primarily a medical or a health issue. It is a social one. Using medical models, then, to "treat" a person labelled "retarded" is as sensible as using a "treatment" for persons who are "athletic" or "talkative." These labels are social judgments. Depending on whom one is with, being "athletic" or "talkative" could be useful, looked down on, irrelevant, or envied. But in any case, would anyone want to "treat" a person for these characteristics?

By looking at persons labelled retarded in terms of their "behavior," we often fail to see who they are or what they want. Our society has recently begun to reexamine its attitudes toward groups of persons it had made marginal. No longer are persons with schizophrenia considered necessarily "sick" nor are elders assumed to be "senile" nor a person with perceptual or motor challenges considered to be a "cripple." It is slowly becoming apparent to others that such persons are quite capable of appreciating their own lives and know what they need to run them.

If persons with schizophrenia from time to time need help in managing reality, if our elders sometimes need help with getting around or in hearing and seeing what is happening, if persons in wheelchairs need special entrances for access, these needs are intrinsic to their conditions—they are not expressions of diminished personality or of a state of lessened and inferior humanity. But as long as we regard their "behavior" as requiring "treatment" or "management," we are failing to integrate them into full membership to our culture. And we have most certainly segregated these persons with state "training schools," "group homes," "nursing homes," "mental hospitals," and so on that lump together persons who are similar because of their differences.

When similar persons all live in one place, it is easier to think of them collectively as a group rather than individually. This is true regardless of whether the place is called a "ward" or "campus" or "ghetto" or "army base." Whenever similar persons live together in large groups, the surrounding culture comes to seem alien. Universities talk about "town and gown" to cover issues affecting both the campus and the community. Municipalities think of "race relations" in dealing with "ghetto" neighborhoods as if those who live in "ghettos" had needs and ambitions the rest of humanity would find hard to understand. Because of this geographic lumping together, each group comes to see the other as somehow different. One dramatic example of this is in Belfast where Protestants know that Catholics smell funny and that Catholics are well aware of how naturally vicious Protestants are. When they come to this country, though, they are seen not as Protestants or Catholics, but "Irish" in a way they do not think of themselves.

Persons labelled retarded have almost always been found in groups, and because of this they have often had their individualities sacrificed. Even in the professional community, there are many examples where such persons have been treated generically rather than individually. (The chief [emeritus] of pediatrics at Duke University in September, 1983, published a statement saying that corrective surgery for children with Down's Syndrome would not help them "because a Down's child is not aware that he is different from others."*

Unfortunately, behavioral therapy is especially suited to maintaining this political disadvantage. Unlike the "talking" therapies, it does not require anything from a person except to be present. Indeed, some behaviorists point out—as an advantage in their style of working with those labelled retarded—how their "treatment" does not require an explanation as to what the plan is intended to do or how and under what conditions it will do it. These "plans" are self-explanatory. But many practitioners have made an unnecessary error of logic with this attitude. Certainly, one does not need to explain to a person the underlying principles of a behavior management plan for it to work. But it does not mean that one ought not do so. Just because we do not have to consider the sensibilities of a person to develop a "behavior plan" does not mean we have compromised anything by doing so. Presumably, the prin-

---

*Ann Landers column, *Boston Globe*, September 9, 1983, p. 57.

ciples of behaviorism apply to those who understand them just as effectively as to those who do not. The real difference is not in the program itself but in the relationship between the person "treating" and the person being "treated" by it.

If I am kept on a locked ward or forbidden to leave a group home on my own or if my insistence that a "treatment program" be changed is ignored, then I am in no way able voluntarily to consent to a "behavioral plan." And what I will have learned, should I try to change my mind, is that the plan can (and often will) forge on without me.

There are some classic "charges" against behaviorism—that it is "heartless," that it is "mind control," that it does not take into account individual freedom and dignity. I think Skinner is correct in seeing these as tangential to his essential argument. Behaviorism has been successful not in developing new ways to "brainwash" unwilling victims so much as it has been of value in identifying and successfully applying the techniques the culture uses anyway. What Skinner has done is to identify and systematically apply these techniques.

There are probably few who do not believe that reinforcement does in fact increase behavior. Indeed, it is impossible not to acknowledge this since the definition of a reinforcer is anything that can be used to increase behavior. This is like the naive "proof" of God's existence: all things come from God because God is the source of all things. This circular logic is one of behaviorism's classical "short suits."

Using any system exclusively limits our understanding of the world. Though some have had local successes, no one religious, philosophical, political, economic, or social system has yet emerged as universally "perfect." Each seems to have a limit. The circular logic that behaviorism uses defines a limit it has as a system: in order to understand *why* a reinforcer increases behavior, we would have to understand *why* the organism "likes" it.

Behaviorism's reliance on strictly empirical (i.e., measurable) information presents the challenge of translating and incorporating its findings into nonempirical social reality. If empirical data were enough, then we would talk only about sex (a more observable and quantifiable phenomenon) but not about love (a nonempirical and unmeasurable subjective state).

Behaviorists, for example, think of feelings as being present at the same time as a stimulus but not necessarily caused by it or causing a change in behavior. For example, touch or eye contact or sexual gratification can lead to a state labelled "love," and when we think we are in this state we can emit behaviors that reinforce others' maintaining touching, looking at us, or gratifying us sexually. But how is it that these fellings are rarely replicated? Has anyone been in love quite the same way twice? To say that it is a matter of different reinforcements and contingencies is just as poor as saying these experiences are different because they are different.

There are, then, many limitations on behaviorism as a theory. The discussion here is just a fragment of the debate that has gone on. But the strength of a theory (to say nothing of persons) is knowing where those limits are. Knowing its theoretical limitations is useful, but knowing its practical limitations is clinically imperative. In practice, behaviorism has demonstrated itself to be a highly effective tool. My goal is to discuss what behaviorism has learned experimentally and how we can apply it practically. It is one thing to know the theoretical physics of internal combustion. It is quite another experience to drive a car.

* * *

Of all the behavioral "techniques," the one I am most comfortable with in theory is satiation, although my experience is that this approach is often used as a way of "one-upping" a person. For example, when I tried to give Martha, the person I mentioned earlier who had constantly sought coffee, all the coffee she could want, I was told, "This is just a satiation program." (I do not understand why it was "just" a satiation program. Did they want more from satiation or from me?) The persons using this program told me things like, "Maybe she'll drink so much coffee, she'll get sick." This was said in a way that suggested her getting sick would not be a bad idea.

My point in working with others is to give them the freedom of choice, the dignity of risk. If they make bad choices that are not seriously dangerous to themselves or others, then perhaps they have learned something. My business is not to control lives. I would not give a person the choice of drinking all the coffee she wants with the goal of getting her sick. The point would be to give her the experience of making her own decisions. So sometimes these ideas have been interpreted as part of a game that will help one "side" of a struggle win over the other.

When others make us uncomfortable, it is information for potential improvement in the way we live, work, and communicate with them. I have noticed that after misunderstandings or even intentional nastiness, that we can have the best opportunity either to build up or to tear down our relationships. When someone makes me uncomfortable and I get a chance to talk it over with that person, the relationship either strengthens or weakens because it has had the chance to grow closer to its emotional and informing truth.

When I read about "treatment programs" that do not take a person's emotional and social needs and responses into account, I feel the sense of lost opportunity. Failure to consider another person's subjective process disappoints me most in the way we sometimes work with others. Everyone has stories, regardless of what sort of work one does, about callousness for the feelings of others. I think that in some circles this sort of insensitivity is considered a mark of accomplishment. There are limits—I hope more everyday—on those who think and act like this.

* * *

One of the classic papers in the development of clinical behavioral practice is Ayllon's (1963) use of satiation with a woman with psychosis.* In some ways, persons with psychosis have differ-

---

*Ayllon T. "Intensive treatment of psychotic behavior by stimulus satiation and food reinforcement." Behavior Research and Therapy, 1983, 1, 53-61. Reprinted with permission of Pergamon Press.

This paper is now over 20 years old. When this paper was written, it demonstrated new hope for persons who had otherwise been written off as "hopeless." At the time, this was a step forward for persons who had been labelled, institutionalized, and often forgotten. Since then, however, many of our attitudes have changed to show greater respect for the dignity of the persons we work with. Too often, though, as Ayllon notes, these changes of awareness have been slow to translate into the day-to-day treatment labelled persons are given.

By analyzing this important paper many years after it was written, however, it is easier to show how today another approach might have been used. It would be ridiculous to suggest that Ayllon was somehow at fault for not having anticipated the next 20 years. My concern is not that Ayllon expresses values that have since changed, but rather that there are those who still use strategies and values that no longer demonstrate respect.

Carroll et al. (1978) said that satiation has gone "virtually unnoticed as a corrective procedure." This is especially true in the literature for persons with handicaps. It seems that as a theoretical process it has been of recurring interest in psychology, particularly in studying eating and sexual behavior. A review of the last five years of Psychological Abstracts shows that papers have been published on satiation using unspecified animals, as well as chickens, sheep, fasted sheep, castrated sheep, male deer mice, pigs, rhesus monkeys, female rabbits, suckling rabbits, quail,

ent challenges from those labelled retarded. But these (and other) groups share, for example, their ostracism from society at large. Regardless of how much is said about the "mainstreaming" of persons with these challenges, they are, for the most part, segregated and discriminated against.

In his introduction Ayllon notes that there has been

> a conspicuous lag between the research findings and their applications. The greatest limitation to the direct application of laboratory principles has been the absence of control over the subjects' environment. Recently, however, a series of applications in a regulated psychiatric setting has clearly demonstrated the possibilities of behavioural modification.... Some of the behaviour studied has included repetitive and highly stereotyped responses such as complaining, pacing, refusal to eat, hoarding and many others.... Specific pathological behaviour patterns of a single patient were treated by manipulating the patient's environment. (p. 53)

Ayllon conducted this series of experiments using "the psychiatric nurses and untrained aides who carried out the environmental manipulations" under his supervision. The environment for these experiments was a locked psychiatric ward for women. The woman upon whom the experiments were carried out was 47 years old and had been "diagnosed as a chronic schizophrenic" who had been hospitalized for nine years. Ayllon found "upon studying the patient's behaviour" that "nursing staff spent a considerable amount of time caring for her." Unfortunately, the way he says it makes it sound—interpreted one way—is that the nurses were somehow imposed upon by having to care for this woman.

Betta splendens, male rats, female rats, suckling rats, weanling rats, rats with gastric fistulas, "obese Ss," male grasshopper mice, college students, obese and lean male mice, macaque monkeys, anorexia nervosa patients, smokers, third and fourth graders, dogs, overeating female Ss, Black neonates, 6–10 year olds, 19–29 year olds, 19–25 year olds, 21–30 year olds, a 37-year-old male, and third to fifth grade males.

There has been no report of Ayllon's findings being adapted into ordinary life for handicapped persons. My own experience has been that those persons using satiation at all do not use it very differently from the way Ayllon did. Woolfolk and Richardson (1984) propose that control is a value that has been implicit to behaviorism. This book proposes that this implicit control can be replaced with a model that explicitly helps all the persons involved in challenging situations to act cooperatively.

Interpreted another way, though, one may think that the nurses felt challenged by her since so much time had been spent in trying to help her.

These challenges were identified as three specific "problem behaviours": stealing food, hoarding the ward's towels in her room, and "her wearing excessive clothing, e.g., a half-dozen dresses, several pairs of stockings, sweaters, and so on." Each of these "problem behaviours" was "treated" in separate experiments.

Often we use assumptions we are unaware of. For example, in this situation, it appears that everyone involved assumed that these "problems" required "treatment." This is quite a different matter from saying that this woman had difficulties and needed help in overcoming them. If I develop a brain tumor, I would turn to one or more experts to treat the tumor. Beyond a basic compliance to their prescriptions, my relationship to these persons could be irrelevant. In working with challenges that are seemingly more cognitive or emotional than physical, I think the relationship between the person helping and the person helped is often a critical variable. I think it is more than just "playing with words" to say that when we "treat" a person, we are putting ourselves in a relationship that is very different (and for me, less desirable) than when we work *with* a person on a challenging situation.

Experiment I:
Control of stealing food by food withdrawal

In the first experiment, Ayllon controlled this woman's food stealing by withdrawing food. By way of background, Ayllon explains that, "the medical staff regarded her excessive weight as detrimental to her health [and] a special diet had been prescribed for her. However, the patient refused to diet and continued stealing food." (p. 54) The "ward staff," he reports, had spent "considerable time trying to persuade her to stop stealing food. As a last resort, the nurses would force her to return stolen food." The nurses watched this woman for a month and determined that she stole food at two-thirds of all meals.

Ayllon's procedure was to stop everyone from trying to use "persuasion, coaxing or coercion." Instead, she was assigned a table in the dining room and no other patients were allowed to sit with her. As Ayllon notes: "Nurses removed the patient from the dining room when she approached a table other than her own, or when she picked up unauthorized food from the dining room counter. In effect, this procedure resulted in the patient missing a meal whenever she attempted to steal food." (p. 54)

The result of this was that "when withdrawal of positive reinforcement (i.e. meal)" was made dependent on the patients "stealing," this response was eliminated in two weeks. Ayllon notes that this patient had never weighed less than 230 pounds during her nine years in hospital and that at the end of this treatment her "weight had stabilized at 180 pounds, or 17 per cent loss from her original weight. At this time, the patient's physical condition was regarded as excellent."

One question that has been a useful starting point for me is, "How does the way a person act help her?" If we start with the assumption that most persons prefer to make themselves comfortable as opposed to uncomfortable, then we can gain some insight into the person's life. If, on the other hand, we start by assuming some things are always good or always bad, then we will end up not in a greater understanding of the person we are working for, but in a struggle to persuade that person that we are right and she is wrong.

This sort of struggle does not seem very attractive to me. Even when it can be won, I wonder if it is a victory worth having. All that can really be won is a type of compliance. I might not agree with what you want me to do, but with the right intimidation I will do it anyway. In the short run, we will appear to be cooperating. But as soon as you stop threatening me, can you trust to my continued goodwill?

For this woman, I wonder if her hoarding and stealing were not her protest against a more general lack of understanding. If she had been asked about a reduction diet and had refused, would her refusal necessarily be a sign of "mental illness" that empowered these persons to overrule her?

I can understand that if a person threatens to harm herself or others that this is considered adequate grounds for taking away certain ordinary freedoms. I am not uncomfortable, in very general terms, with the idea of restraining a person who wants to destroy herself since many times this is a brief conviction. I would be willing to try to talk a person away from a bottle of pills or a loaded gun. But we have to make a distinction between specific actions that will result in destruction and lifestyles that will. Do we feel empowered to take all those who smoke, drink excessively, overeat, or refuse medical treatment for treatable diseases and lock them

up? It is not that I care too little about the lives of others that
makes me want to leave them alone, but that I care too much. If
someone chooses a chronic and debilitating way to live, I am re-
signed to thinking it wiser to respect that and try only to make that
choice as informed as possible.

So when this woman weighs more than is generally thought
to be healthy, we are faced with a delicate consideration. Just because she has episodes of psychosis, does it mean that she cannot
make other decisions rationally? Again, I am making the distinction between a person who has lost contact with reality and demands, for example, to be fed nothing but glass and a person who
habitually eats ordinary food to excess.

It was not Ayllon's point to discuss how these decisions were
made; so it is not intended as a criticism of his work that he did
not. Certainly, Ayllon did nothing very different ethically than is
commonly done even now. But I wonder if these well-intentioned
goals could not have been achieved with different means. If this
woman, for instance, said, "I would rather die than diet," then if
we respect her decision we have the basis for establishing some
mutual respect. This would make it possible for us to establish a
trusting relationship so that if she did change her mind she would
feel it was her decision and not ours. It is also possible, as I say,
that she would in fact die from complications of her excessive
weight.

This is not an easy issue that can be lightly resolved, though
I think the resolution of this should leave all of the participants in
it with some sense of respect for one another. But I do not see how
we could approach this woman respectfully by telling her that by
reason of her psychosis she would have to lose weight—which is
what we would be saying. Only her episodes of psychosis would
lead to her being admitted to a psychiatric hospital, and if she were
not a psychiatric patient, there would be no way anyone could legally compel her to diet.

All this implies that the way this decision was made immediately established a relationship between unequal parties. I think
there is some essential violation of our cultural training when we
do this. Even if our society is not always fair to everyone, many
take comfort that we are trying to reach that ideal. But there are
some situations that will allow others to act contrary to their ordinary feelings. For instance, Stanley Milgram (1964) found that
persons directed by an "authority" during an experiment would
administer what they thought were painful levels of electric shock

if told the "authority" would assume responsibility.* I think what we do as "scientists" can obscure what we do as individual persons. Sometimes we can justify the inconvenience of our second thoughts if an experiment is sufficiently "scientific." So while behaviorism has introduced the concept of empirical validation into the study of human behavior, it has also drawn attention to data rather than process. I think it is an unnecessary sacrifice: one can be respectful of another person and at the same time use independent measures to show progress or lack of it in what we do.

In this experiment, the fact that the woman's weight had dropped to 180 pounds is taken as validation that the program "worked." This reliance on a number is questionable. Why 180? Would it have worked better if she had reached 175 pounds or less well at 185 pounds? When "the medical staff" decided that this "patient" was overweight, on what did they base their decision?

Again, if we first ask how the way a person acts is adaptive for her, we can come to a more complete understanding of this and to a way of helping her change it. It is hard to do this if we ignore what she does. So paying no attention to her stealing food is an effective way of saying, "We don't know why you do this and we don't care." If she were hungry on the diet—many of us on diets

---

*In discussing Milgram's experiments on ways that consensus opinion can influence individuals, Krech et al. (1974) note that "the individual goes along with the group, apparently irrespective of his true (though unknown) inclinations." They conclude their discussion by quoting from Harold Laski's essay (1929), "The Dangers of Obedience":

Civilization means, above all, an unwillingness to inflict unnecessary pain. Within the ambit of that definition, those of us who heedlessly accept the commands of authority cannot yet claim to be civilized men . . . our business, if we desire to live a life not utterly devoid of meaning and significance, is to accept nothing which contradicts out basic experience merely because it comes from tradition or convention or authority. If may well be that we shall be wrong; but our self-expression is thwarted at the root unless the certainties we are asked to accept coincide with the certainties we experience. That is why the condition of freedom in any state is always a widespread and consistent skepticism of the canons upon which power insists.

I assume, this strong challenge is as true for ourselves as the persons we work with.

are—then her stealing was a sensible way of relieving this discomfort. Since she had been stealing food before this experiment had begun, though, one might suspect that this was one strategy she used in engaging others socially. One can imagine that the persons she stole food from did not ignore this behavior and the persons working in the dining room in turn would speak to her about this. If stealing food were her most effective way of socializing, then she would profit from learning to be more cooperative. Of course, this is just a guess. The best way to understand this behavior would be to ask her about it. Unfortunately, it is easier to look at another person's decisions and discount them than it is to try to understand the logic and even the necessity behind them.

In this case, one wonders what this woman was thinking and feeling. How many persons not under lock and key would have tolerated this program? She had already refused voluntarily to diet; so other than "stealing," how could she have effectively protested her being placed on an unwanted diet?

The plan's "withdrawal of a positive reinforcement (i.e. meal)" also raises some questions as to how this woman understood this program. If we define a meal as a reinforcer, then this constitutes a punishment program. If this interpretation of events is correct—that she did not want to diet, that she was hungry because of this unwanted reduction in food, and that she stole from hunger—then this plan in effect punishes her for our decisions. Again, this is an effective tool, but I am concerned about the application of it. Performing this experiment in the social isolation of a locked ward allows one to overlook that this intervention is very like the common child-rearing practice of disciplining children by sending them to bed without a meal.

> Because the patient was not informed or warned of the consequences that followed stealing, the nurses regarded the procedure as unlikely to have much effect on the patient's behaviour. The implicit belief that verbal instructions are indispensable for learning is part of present-day psychiatric lore. In keeping with this notion, prior to this behaviour treatment, the nurses tried to persuade the patient to co-operate in dieting. Because there were strong medical reasons for her losing weight, the patient's refusal to follow the prescribed diet was regarded as further evidence of her mental illness. (p. 56)

I think our goal in working with others is to help them prepare for as normal a life as they can live. My preference is to do this through modeling. I try to talk to everyone as appropriately as I can, extending the same consideration and courtesy as best my imperfect self allows. A program like Ayllon's would give me little opportunity to do this. Instead, I would constantly have to *react* to what this woman was doing rather than *interact*. I think the give and take of working with others is not only useful in working effectively, but it is also fun. When a person does something, I am not uncomfortable asking what it means to her. If she finds acting that way uncomfortable, then I look for ways she can learn another way. My experience is that this allows me to build a working relationship rather than exert my trained will on a "problem behavior."

I think this woman's reluctance to diet can be interpreted for reasons other than "mental illness." Her weight might well have been a health hazard, but we pick and choose which health hazards offend us. Smoking has its well-documented and harmful effects on health. Could a similar program have been instituted for all the smokers living and working at the hospital? Certainly. Could it have been done under the same conditions, that is, without the express cooperation of the persons involved? Certainly not. Would we consider it a sign of "mental illness" every time someone lights a cigarette? We might. And if we did, would we feel empowered to forbid them cigarettes? Again, we might but only until we actually tried to take the cigarettes from those persons who wanted them.

A plan such as Ayllon's seems well suited to teaching the concept of respect for authority, but I think this lesson is less useful, hence less desirable, than an approach that taught through demonstration respect for oneself and for others.

Experiment II: Control of one form of hoarding behavior through stimulus satiation

The same woman had been hoarding towels in her room for her nine years of hospitalization. Despite efforts by her care givers to discourage this, she continued so that twice a week others would remove them from her room. To determine the degree to which she engaged in this, some persons would go into her room when she was not present and count the number of towels, which ranged from 19 to 29 despite the fact that they were being removed several times a week.

Ayllon's intervention was to stop taking the towels away:

Instead, a programme of stimulus satiation was carried out by the nurses. Intermittently, throughout the day, the nurses took a towel to the patient and simply handed it to her without any comment. The first week, she was given an average of 7 towels daily, and by the third week this number was increased to 60.

During the first few weeks of satiation, the patient was observed patting her cheeks with a few towels, apparently enjoying them. Later, the patient was observed spending much of her time folding and stacking the approximately 600 towels in her room. A variety of remarks were made by the patient regarding receipt of towels. All verbal statements made by the patient were recorded by the nurse. The following represent typical remarks made during this experiment. First week: As the nurse entered the patient's room carrying a towel, the patient would smile and say, "Oh, you found it for me, thank you." Second week: when the number of towels given to the patient increased rapidly, she told the nurses, "Don't give me no more towels. I've got enough." Third week: "Take them towels away.... I can't sit here all night and fold towels." Fourth and fifth week: "Get these dirty towels out of here." Sixth week: After she had started taking towels out of her room, she remarked to the nurse, "I can't drag any more of these towels, I just can't do it!"

The quality of these remarks suggests that the initial effect of giving towels to the patient was reinforcing. However as the towels increased they ceased to be reinforcing, and presumably became aversive. (pp. 56–7)

Ayllon and the persons working with him set out to demonstrate how powerful behavioral strategies could be even without a person's understanding them or wanting to cooperate with them. In this they succeeded. Unfortunately, though, many persons have taken this as a cue to continue this pattern of socially isolating persons who are already socially isolated. It is difficult to guess what this woman wanted from her hoarding towels. Given this, one would like to establish a relationship with her that would begin to give us some explanation as to how she sees this as adaptive. Rather than going into her room and counting the towels while she was gone, it might be helpful just to ask her directly. The plan presented in this experiment avoids opportunities to talk with this woman, to establish a relationship, and act as if one were genuinely attempting to be helpful. It is worth remembering that when Ayllon did this series of experiments, it was thought that a person's cooperation and "insight" into "treatment" was imperative. For experimental purposes, then, his consistent refusal to develop "insight" makes an important point in our understanding of how behavior can be shaped. But knowing we can shape behavior without involving the person herself does not mean we can provide better service that way. It only establishes that it is unnecessary to tell someone why she has to change in order for her to do so.

Sometimes it is useful to ask what we intend to achieve with our interventions. Do we expect to teach this woman how little we think of her hoarding and how we can make it unpleasant? Or do we want her to get to the point where she can say, "This is no longer necessary for me; I'd rather do something else with my time"?

I think it could have been more effective to say, "I don't understand why you need these towels but we have lots of them here and if you need them, take them." This would have given her a chance to satiate on the towels as a stimulus, but it would also have given her a chance to discuss what all this meant to her. There are many plausible reasons for her hoarding: she was bored, lonely, amused at seeing others having to cart her towels away. It might have been more effective if someone had asked her and learned what these reasons were.

Suppose she had confided after a while, "The towels are nothing to me except to help break up boredom." Persons confined to a locked ward typically have very little to do and even less that is pleasant to see or hear or smell.

Or suppose she just liked towels because they were soft and pleasant to hold. She could, perhaps, have been offered a job in a laundry (most hospitals have one) where she could have had access to handling many towels a day but in a useful job. The benefits to this intervention would have been more immediately generalized to the rest of her life. She would have had the opportunity to see herself as a woman with a job rather than a patient with "mental illness"; she could have had access to talking with others. Her experience in such a job might also be useful in gaining employment once she was able to leave the hospital. These are only suggestions based on reasons she might have given. These examples are intended to show the sort of cooperation one could realistically extend to her based on what *she* tells us rather than waiting for the cooperation she might have to give based on what *we* tell her.

With Ayllon's plan I am uncertain as to what message this woman may have received. What did she think when others insisted on giving her towels when she asked them not to? How did her enjoyment of folding the towels get overlooked as a good starting point for teaching her? This plan raises a question that we often avoid: how do we handle our frustration and anger with those who—despite our best efforts—do not change? Few of us enjoy feeling ineffective, but many persons pose challenges that make us feel inadequate. Sometimes these feelings lead to abuse, some of it blatant, some of it subtle. My concern is that the persons working with this woman felt she was beyond their abilities to help. While this plan was well thought out and demonstrated a logical finding of psychology, I wonder if the authors were calling this a plan of "stimulus satiation," while the woman herself was calling it "revenge"?

Experiment III: Control of an additional form of hoarding through food reinforcement

Shortly after the patient had been admitted to the hospital, she wore an excessive amount of clothing which included several sweaters, shawls, dresses, undergarments and stockings. The clothing also included sheets and towels wrapped around her body, and a turban-like head-dress made up of several towels. In addition, the patient carried two to three cups in one hand while holding a bundle of miscellaneous clothing, and a large purse on the other. (p. 58)

Could this way of acting have been a reasonable solution to an unreasonable situation for this woman? Persons who have not lived or worked in a "mental hospital" might have no idea as to what it can be like. Even today, it usually is not like going to a general hospital. For example, one rarely has a place for personal possessions; so if you want to keep something, you carry it. When your clothes go to the laundry, they often do not come back. You are given to wear what is available from a common supply. Understandably, if you find something comfortable, you keep wearing it. Often there are problems in institutions because some persons will hoard clothing or refuse to take if off when it is dirty. One can well imagine a 38-year-old woman coming to such a hospital from a home where she had her own closets and bureau. One normal reaction would be to cling to those things that seemed most worth keeping.

So if one starts wearing two shirts on Monday, one might well be wearing five by Thursday. The original premise—save what you want to keep—makes sense, but it gets extended to the point where it makes the person look unusual. By the time this woman was wearing 18 pairs of stockings, it was only a small step toward completing this ensemble with a turban of towels. What this woman was doing could have started as a logical solution to a real problem. What could easily have happened was that she perseverated to the point where her solution was causing more problems than it solved.

Persons who live in institutions often perseverate. Sometimes this is an expression of an organic disorder; other times, it reflects an adaptation to the environment. Life in a psychiatric hospital often alternates between being boring and frightening. One common way to make a turbulent and unpredictable environment more acceptable is to develop rituals or hang on to objects that are either safe, comforting, or familiar. In this environment her many layers of clothing might have provided a sense of safety for her, and putting them on every day might have been a reassuring ritual. Whether this *was* the reason for her dressing as she did cannot be determined. She, of course, would be in a better position to tell us than for us to tell her about that. But it is the sort of speculation that would help us better understand that she might have good reason for her actions. So if this were the case, then we could work out an agreement with her to help her with this. Rather than focusing on her "behavior," we could invest our energies in removing the need for it. If she had been given a place to store her garments and access to a washing machine, she could have kept them clean and safe and not have needed to wear them all the time in order to keep them.

To determine how much clothing she was wearing, she was weighed before going into the dining room for two weeks. During that time the amount of clothing was determined by subtracting her body weight from the weight obtained. The procedure was to make her meals contingent on her weight. At the beginning, she was allowed 23 pounds above her actual body weight to get a meal. Since she regularly wore about 25 pounds of clothing, this meant she had to wear two pounds less than usual to eat. If she weighed more than her body weight plus the amount allowed for clothing,

> the nurse stated in a matter-of-fact manner, "Sorry, you weigh too much, you'll have to weigh less." Failure to meet the required weight resulted in the patient missing a meal at which she was being weighed. . . . Some verbal shaping was done in order to encourage the patient to leave the cups and bundles she carried with her. Nurses stopped her at the dining room and said, "Sorry, no things are allowed in the dining room." No mention of cloth-

ing or specific items was made to avoid focusing undue attention upon them. (p. 58)

During the initial part of this experiment, the patient showed some emotional behaviour, e.g., crying, shouting and throwing chairs around. Because nurses were instructed to "ignore" this emotional behaviour, the patient obtained no sympathy or attention from them. The withholding of social reinforcement for emotional behaviour quickly led to its elimination. . . .

About this time the patient's parents came to visit her and insisted on taking her home for a visit. This was the first time during the patient's 9 years of hospitalization that her parents had asked to take her out. They remarked that previously they had not been interested in taking her out because the patient's excessive dressing in addition to her weight made her look like "a circus freak. . . . (p. 59)

The patient displayed some emotional behaviour in each experiment, but each time it subsided when social reinforcement (i.e. attention) was not forthcoming. The patient did not become violent or seclusive as a consequence of these experiments. Instead, she became socially more accessible to patients and staff. She did not achieve a great deal of social success but she did begin to participate actively in social functions. (p. 60)

It is here that I think the messages this woman was getting were most confused and least likely to help her in living independently of a hospital. Living independently means being able to make one's own decisions, to choose to do things because they make life simpler or more pleasant rather than because one has no choice. Certainly, ordinary living involves a number of chores about which we have little choice, but the problems addressed in this experiment are not those sorts of tasks. We can choose to an extent how much we want to weigh; we choose what we keep in our rooms; we choose what we wear. None of these issues would necessarily lead to a person's being institutionalized. Doing any of these things in a manner too far from social norms leaves us at risk for being labelled "eccentric" or "crazy," but they are harmless to society. Instead of insisting that this woman change because *we* would think it more normal, it would have been more to the point to give her the opportunities to see how differently she acted than most other persons. This is a hard point to make on a locked ward for persons with psychosis.

One of behaviorism's great contributions to clinical psychology is the idea that the problem is not in the person; it is in the environment. This takes the burden from trying to reorganize a person's

(invisible) psychological structure and provides the rationale for giving the person a new environment to learn new skills. One simple
intervention would have been to work around or overlook the unusual things this woman did and take her to more normal places.
I have discussed how these apparently odd habits could have made
sense in the unusual environment of a psychatric ward. I would
have a harder time making sense of them in a more normal environment. My premise is that this woman would have as difficult
a time as I would in finding how they would be helpful to her outside of a psychiatric hospital. In a more ordinary environment, if
she changed at all she would be more likely to change in a more
conventional direction.

My interest in this sort of intervention would not be to make
this woman "normal." My interest would be in helping her find
how to be comfortable in "normal" society. If she were to go into
a public place dressed as Ayllon described her, then she would
most probably be treated with rudeness or ridicule at worst and
awkwardly avoided at best. This could make her sufficiently uncomfortable to want to change provided she was sensitive to a social environment. We sometimes forget that knowing how to have
relationships is learned; they are not simply instinctual. When a
person acts "bizarrely," this is often the result of her being unaware of the social consequences or being frightened about how to
manage any social situation successfully. This is a skills deficit we
commonly overlook, perhaps because it is so obvious. But we need
to consider these possibilities for a working relationship with her.
A better understanding of her social goals and functioning could
help us work with her accordingly. This would put us in the position of being resources for information and support rather than being seen as controlling and confrontative.

One wonders if, in this kind of helping relationship, she would
not eventually be more comfortable asking us how we thought she
looked. We could then answer honestly that she looked different.
When a person feels as alienated from the general culture as persons labelled psychotic, or retarded (or even adolescent), often feel,
then we frequently see this sense of alienation reflected in their
"antisocial" behavior and "bizarre" dress. Gradually, as one feels
herself to be a respected member of a larger community, she begins to dress and act more in accordance with community stan-
dards. One of the difficulties I feel while reading Ayllon's study is
that these experiments presume that the ways persons act are independent of their own sense of adaptation and responsibility.

> The research presented here was conducted under nearly ideal conditions. The variables manipulated (i.e., towels and food) were under full experimental control . . . . The results. . .indicate that none of the three pathological behaviour patterns (i.e., food stealing, hoarding, and excessive dressing) exhibited by the patient were replaced by any undersirable behaviour. (p. 60)

Ayllon's purpose was best served by working under "full experimental control." How else could he have established that his hypothesis worked for the reasons he said it did and no other? But the problem with this research is that while it satisfies an academic standard it does not meet a social need. The problems this woman had were in learning to control herself. These experiments showed ways we could learn better to control *her*. This is a starting point 180 degrees from my own: that we do not have the right to decide for others what they have to change. We have the privilege of helping them change if they ask us to, in whatever ways they can. But because some persons have a label such as "psychotic" or "reatrded," it is easy and traditional to think they also can only do "psychotic" or "retarded" things.

> A frequent problem encountered in mental hospitals is overeating. In general this problem is solved by prescribing a reduction diet. Many patients, however, refuse to take a reduction diet and continue overeating. When confronted by this behaviour, psychiatric workers generally resort to two types of explanations. . . .
>
> One explanation of overeating points out that only with the active and sincere cooperation of the patient can weight reduction be accomplished. When the patient refuses to cooperate he is regarded as showing more signs of mental illness and all hopes of eliminating overeating come to an end.
>
> Another type of explanation holds that overeating is not the behaviour to be concerned with. Instead, attention is focused on the psychological "needs" of the patient. These "needs" are said to be the cause of the observable behaviour, overeating. Therefore the emphasis is on the removal of the cause and not the symptom or behaviour itself. Whatever theoretical merit these explanations may have, it is unfortunate that they fail to suggest practical ways of treating this behaviour itself. As a consequence, the patient continues to overeat often to the detriment of his health. (p. 60)

Again, this assumes that, when persons with schizophrenia, for example, do something, what they are doing is necessarily "schizophrenic." If, and I admit it happens, I occasionally eat excessive amounts of food, is that pathological? Even if it could possibly be so, would it help in any way to call it that? By labelling a behavior, we now have a behavior with a label and not a plan to help anyone with it.

My differences with Ayllon's experiment fall into neither of the two categories he sees. I understand that one does not need "the active and sincere cooperation" of a person to effect weight change. Depriving a person of her meals will effectively do this. Nor is my reservation that this will frustrate a deep-seated psychological "need" for food. Instead, it will frustrate the person's acquiring social resources that will help her learn how to get support for the decisions she herself makes.

My focusing on "psychological needs" is not the same sense of the term as used in depth psychology. By "psychological needs," I am thinking of ordinary, day-to-day benefits that living cooperatively with others can provide.

* * *

Donald is a man in his early twenties who has been labelled profoundly retarded (one IQ estimate placed his at 14). He wears glasses with thick lenses and walks hunched slightly forward as if he were trying to carry something without anyone's seeing. He is nonverbal, which further gives the impression of someone who is withdrawn and difficult to communicate with.

He has caused some concern at his training program because he has been leaving the toilet with his pants around his ankles. When he is alone in the toilet, he apparently has been shredding toilet paper or hoarding toilet paper in his pants so he can shred it later. At first, some thought he might be confused about where he was or absentmindedly was not pulling his pants up. But in his previous training program, he had been forbidden to shred things (the other program had a "behavioral plan" for this "problem"). The only place he could find to shred without "consequences" was the toilet; so if someone else came in, the first thing he did was to hide the paper he was shredding so as to avoid punishment. This often meant that he did not have time to pull his pants up.

His first choice of shredding material was socks. This had been enough of a problem at home that the persons there would reprimand him for shredding anything because it usually meant that he had stolen socks. But a program to forbid him from shredding both where he worked and where he lived had not been successful. Instead of stopping, he tried to be more discreet. Since he had difficulty in seeing, this made him fearful of being near others. It also made him act in a way that some others called sneaky.

Those who worked with Donald tried to understand why shredding might be satisfying to him. Perhaps it was his way of relaxing; another person with more sophisticated skills might take up knitting in the way he had taken up shredding. In any case, it was obviously important enough for him to steal to do it.

Our first step was to recognize that somehow Donald found this shredding helpful. Since it is common for some persons to fidget with things like coins or their pens, we thought he might find the same satisfaction in a more socially acceptable substitute. Donald went shopping with this suggestion and picked out a key chain with a brightly colored Rubik's cube on it. He played with this for a while, but he continued to steal socks for shredding; so this substitute was obviously not as satisfying for him.

Since telling him that shredding was unacceptable behavior seemed to have no impact, it was easy to see that he did not feel enough of a sense of community to respond to social pressure. My first interest was for Donald to see others as helpful and friendly rather than as spies he constantly had to avoid. Most of the persons who worked with him preferred to think of themselves as helpers rather than as private detectives, which made it easier to get their cooperation in this endeavor.

We decided that of all the "socially unacceptable" things a person could do, shredding was a fairly harmless choice. It did not appear to be ordinary behavior, but our goal was to help Donald make a choice,* rather than forcing him to accept what we thought best. By having tried social pressure and failed, we had made social con-

---

*Persons who are identified as different have fewer choices of what they can do than persons who are already incorporated into mainstream culture. As Marc Gold (1980) noted, the more competence a person has, the more society will tolerate an apparent deviance. When Rosie Grier took up needlepoint, he was able to use his considerable status as a football player to show that needlepoint can be a useful and relaxing hobby for anyone who finds it relaxing and useful. If those who have been labelled retarded (or labelled another way that identifies them as being different) were to do the same thing, it would only serve to make them appear more different and even more easily dismissed. Dr. Gold, a leader in the field of training persons who find it difficult to learn, developed the "Try Another Way" method of teaching and in the training manual for that approach discusses further the competency-deviancy hypothesis.

siderations even less important for him. So our goal was to establish ourselves as friendly helpers. This would be the first step in encouraging him to feel part of a social group without feeling threatened by it. We decided that the quickest way to appear less threatening was to stop making threats.

Anyone who does laundry is well acquainted with one of the twentieth century's more vexing riddles: what happens to socks when they are washed? Why does only one from each pair disappear? And where to?

Rather than force Donald to steal, he was given a supply of socks whose mates had disappeared. To help him feel he did not need to hide them, he was told to keep the socks wherever he wanted so that he could get as many as he needed whenever he needed them. At work he was told that he could shred whenever he had free time. Some of us felt that it would not be reasonable to encourage him to choose shredding over working but that he should have access to both. The first goal was to reduce his anxiety about having the socks at all and then to reduce his anxiety about shredding them.

There was some problem initially in doing this. Some persons felt that he should not shred while he was in church or in restaurants since these were inappropriate places for such activity. But it was precisely because these places were inappropriate that we could afford temporarily to overlook his shredding. He had learned that the only reason to stop shredding things was that others had told him to stop; he had not learned to take cues from the environment as to when shredding would be appropriate and when it would not. Our attitude was to be neutral about his decision. This would mean that he would have to decide for himself when it was appropriate to shred and when not, and it would give him the opportunity to learn this the same way most of us do: by observing the environment and the ways others acted in it. Since others had tried to point these social factors out to him in the past and this effort had been unsuccessful, we thought that continuing to repeat this would only make us and not his shredding the issue.

The approach that everyone then used was, "We don't understand why you need to do this, but if it helps you then we want to help." Because he had been reprimanded and nagged about his shredding so much in the past, we were careful to show Donald how much we really meant what we said. We were concerned, at least initially, that if we set conditions on his shredding, he would see this as a kind of trick.

As for his hoarding, the approach we decided to use was one

of reminding him to use his pockets. Some persons found themselves saying, "You don't need to hide that in your socks, you can keep it in your pockets. But it's up to you."

And finally, we will return to the original problem—his walking around with his pants down around his ankles. The persons working with Donald were able to persuade him that his shredding caused them so little concern that he did not have to hide in the bathroom to do it. Once this was established, if another person came into the toilet, Donald did not have to panic and could redress himself like anyone else.

These, of course, were only beginning steps. The goal was to place shredding in a more ordinary social context. Our hope was that once he no longer felt shredding was unique, that he would be able to get the same satisfaction from similar activities, he could then expand his range of choices. When shredding was no longer an issue, the next step would be to offer him substitute activities that might serve the same function without identifying him even more as "different" the way shredding had done. The key chain with the Rubik's cube could then be reintroduced, and because it was something relatively new, he might even prefer it to the shredding. Someone knew of a kit to make place mats with frayed edges. These later steps were to be offered after Donald was confident that his need to shred was respected. If he later decided that he would prefer something else, he could choose it. But he would not be forced to do so.

This plan differs from the standard "satiation" programs in subtle, but I think important, ways. Here, the goal is not to use social attention as a reinforcer; instead, social attention is a given. The goal here is primarily to help Donald understand others better by seeing them as a resource and not as an obstacle to be worked around. In that sense, if he had never given up shredding but was comfortable being with others, then this way of working would have been a partial success. The point of this plan is not to eliminate a "behavior." The point is to improve his quality of life by integrating him into the community in which he lives and works. By respecting his wishes, other persons were modeling ways in which he might respect theirs. My goal was to give him the basis for improving his trust and relationships.

Six weeks later, Donald had stopped stealing socks altogether. When one of the persons he lived with dropped a sock on her way from the laundry room, Donald picked it up and brought it to her. Perhaps Donald is now helping us answer one of the twentieth century's great unsolved mysteries.

Postscript

In spite of my never calling it this, the persons who worked at Donald's home called this intervention a "behavioral plan." And in spite of my emphasizing what I thought to be the social aspects of this approach, the real target for them was eliminating his shredding. My point has been that we usually cannot change just one thing in a person's life without rearranging other things as well. This assumption is one I try to exploit in working out a system for a person to learn new strategies. Nonetheless, persons who are trained to look at "behaviors" as they occur rather than at the systems in which they take place can have a difficult time in grasping the idea that skills generalize. Several weeks after Donald's problem had been declared "resolved," I met with some of the persons who worked with him.

"Donald made a real breakthrough last night," they told me.

"How?" I asked, happy to hear that things were still progressing.

"Well, we hadn't told you but Donald couldn't do his laundry without standing next to the machine. Even though he knew he was not living in an institution, he was still convinced that someone would come and steal his clothes."

I thought this really was a step toward Donald's feeling a part of ordinary society and that he had started to learn how to trust others on some basic issues of daily life. I then made a little joke to the effect that sometimes psychologists actually have ideas that work.

"What do you mean?" they asked. "How did your program with the socks have anything to do with it?"

Satiation and Some Other Behavioral Strategies

The common charges against behaviorism—that it is "heartless" or "controlling"—are based more on the application of the principles than on the principles themselves. The reason for this, I think, is that the behavioral literature has been more interested in establishing what works experimentally than in exploring how to make it work in socially normal settings. Ayllon's paper, for example, establishes how satiation can be an effective intervention. What he does not discuss is how it can be effective in ordinary settings. It is hardly fair to criticize an author or authors for not considering every implication of their work. It is, however, worth reviewing the literature on satiation in terms of how these interventions could be adapted to a nonexperimental environment.

Carroll et al. (1978) note that "satiation has gone virtually unnoticed as a corrective procedure" (p. 248) and that:

> Past research has restricted the technique of satiation to behaviors such as magazine hoarding (Ayllon and Michael, 1959) and towel hoarding (Ayllon, 1963) and...the positive practice overcorrection dressing procedure which Foxx (1976) used with disrobers.... (p. 248)
>
> Some [emotionally disturbed, mentally retarded] individuals are apparantly [sic] reinforced by having an item of clothing to tear (Baumeister & Klosowski, 1965) and this trait combined with the fact that clothes ripping behavior usually receives the immediate attention of direct care staff creates a situation in which clothes ripping can easily be maintained. (p. 246)

I think it is useful to understand as best we can the assumptions we make in our work. In this case, we are really assuming that a "behavior" continues only when "reinforced." I think, given the circular definitions of these terms, that this is undeniably true. But we run into a problem when we assume what reinforces a behavior. Sometimes what appears to be a cause and effect relationship is literally only a coincidence. For example, it would be a mistake to assume that because every time I take a bath the phone rings that the phone reinforces my "bath-taking behavior." It is only a coincidence. So if every time one of these persons shreds something and someone else comes along, their comments on it might reinforce "shredding behavior." But without data to support this hypothesis, we can only guess that. Just as in the case of my taking a leisurely soak, this shredding may be reinforcing in and of itself to the person alone.

"Staff attention," in my experience, is a commonly attempted reinforcer. I am not certain what this means, although my understanding of it is that it involves talking to someone as a person rather than as a "client" or a "resident" or a "patient." I wonder if this sort of social exchange is more effective when it is made formal and contingent. Or would we develop a more comfortable working relationship with a person if this style of conversation were not just the way things are?

The six men chosen for a study by Carroll and his colleagues (1978) ranged in age from 19 to 32 years and had been institutionalized from 8 to 29 years.

Four of the six subjects showed high rates of aggressive, disruptive behavior and posed frequent management problems for the aide staff. Prior to the study, these subjects had been placed in time out for 15 minutes after ripping and were redressed by staff after the time out period had ended. The subjects were randomly assigned to three groups of two subjects each for the study . . . (p. 247)

Treatment consisted of three parts: satiation, over-correction, and a DRO [differential reinforcement of other behavior] schedule of reinforcement.

Satiation and overcorrection were immediate consequences of the ripping behavior while the DRO schedule was in effect throughout the treatment phase.

After each occurrence of the ripping behavior, the resident was taken to a time out room and instructed to sit with his back to the wall. . . .

. . .He was then handed the garment he had previously ripped and was told to rip, to continue ripping, the material to the smallest possible pieces. The satiation procedure continued for 15 minutes and was followed by the overcorrection procedure which required the resident to dress and undress repeatedly for 15 minutes. If at any time during the satiation or overcorrection, the resident resisted making the desired movements, he was "shadowed" until he performed the procedure independently. Shadowing, a procedure described by Foxx and Azrin (1972) required that the residents' [sic] hands be taken by the experimenter and gently but firmly guided until he was ripping or dressing on his own. Shadowing was also used to assure a relatively constant rate in the desired movement. If, during the over-correction procedure, the resident ripped, or attempted to rip again, the procedure was reinitiated beginning with the satiation procedure.

In order further to weaken the response of ripping, reinforcement was provided on a DRO schedule for all nondisruptive behavior. Reinforcements were candy treats (M&M's, caramel, chews, *etc.*) presented with a great deal of social reinforcement (verbal praise accompanied by patting the resident or shaking his hand). At first, reinforcers were presented after 10 minutes of clothes wearing. After an hour of non-ripping, the interval between reinforcers was increased to 20 minutes. After 2 hours of success on the DRO 20 minute schedule, the length of time required to receive reinforcements was increased to 45 minutes. . . . (p. 248)

In some ways, this appears to use the technique of the paradoxical therapists who *insist* a person keep doing exactly the sort of things we would ordinarily wish they would stop. But the effect these two approaches create are in opposite directions.

Using paradoxical therapy, Viktor Frankl, for example, once asked a man frightened of elevators what would happen if he got into one. The man was afraid of fainting and looking foolish. Trusting that the man would not, indeed probably could not, do this, Frankl took him into the elevator. To the man's surprise and relief, he felt uncomfortable but nowhere near fainting. This sort of approach sometimes looks a little odd except, as I say, the end point is that the person can learn from experience that what had plagued him is no longer an emotional psychological reality. This man now feels at liberty to use or avoid elevators as he chooses.

If paradoxical instruction typically takes a behavior or attitude a person finds aversive and makes it go away, overcorrection takes something a person enjoys—or at least does frequently—and makes it aversive. This is sometimes used with children who want to smoke. Parents agree to their children's smoking on the condition they smoke an entire pack of cigarettes or several strong cigars. Predictably, such children get sick and learn that smoking is a sickening experience. Neither paradox nor overcorrection is a "good" or a "bad" idea any more than a knife is a "good" or a "bad" utensil. It is the social context in which these things are used that makes them helpful or questionable.

In this case, the "subjects" were not children needing guidance from their parents. And they had not asked anyone to help them with their ripping. This does not mean that the persons working with them should have just shrugged it off. Ripping clothing might have some soothing effect on the person doing it, but it is not a skill that will be helpful to these men if they try to live in an ordinary environment. But because they seem to want to do it, we must start from a different place than if they asked us to help them change. If we do not present ourselves as trustworthy helpers, then we will find ourselves ultimately in the position of saying, "You will stop ripping" and their saying, "Make me." This sort of struggle has no winners. So if this process of change is undesirable, I think it better to begin immediately with ways that will make change acceptable.

One way would be to offer to these men the opportunity to shred at specific times or places with rags. This would remove the struggle of trying to stop it altogether but at the same time present those persons as helping by offering reasonable alternatives.

There are some understandable reservations about this sort of approach. One is that it seems too sophisticated for persons labelled severely or profoundly retarded. One might reasonably ask, "How can I negotiate with someone who can't talk?" The answer is through trial and error. If we explain what we are trying to do to others, they may or may not give the appearance of understanding, but if we then go ahead and start to use some plan with them, they will certainly show through their actions whether they want to cooperate or not. This sort of give-and-take lets us know how others feel about our work. When we offered Gregory a mat to lie on, he would smile and give the impression that he enjoyed the chance to take a break. But even if he gave no facial expression, his learning to use the mat to give himself a change would have showed he "agreed" with the new plan. As for this approach being too sophisticated, my experience is that this is not the case. Most of my own work has been with persons who have been labelled as severely or profoundly retarded, and while I have been challenged to find effective ways of negotiation, I have not (yet) encountered a situation where this was impossible.

Another objection is that this approach seems time consuming and cumbersome. A "behavioral plan" can fix things up more quickly and usually produces data that clearly demonstrates success or the lack of it. This may or may not be true. I have not compared this approach with "behavior plans" enough to know if this is true or not. But if we consider that the persons we work with usually have been having difficulties for some time, then we can hardly expect to make a sudden and effective change for them. If we think that these persons and their challenges have often been given quick solutions (such as being brushed off, or "bought off" to keep them from complaining too noisily), this approach has a novelty for them: someone is listening and asking them what they want rather than just trying to placate them or smooth things over.

I think any approach that enhances a person's sense of value and dignity is worth a lifetime of trying. Most of us do not always have perfect relationships. The challenge and the testimony to the ones we love is that in spite of difficulty—even the occasional feeling of hopelessness—we continue to try to make a real relationship closer to an ideal one.

Finally, this seems to ask that we just learn to accept others the way they are. This is my least intention. I think seeing a person who cannot live or act independently and just accepting that is condescending and cruel. Rather than debating *if* change is possible, I am interested in seeing *how* change can be made effectively. I am expecially concerned that the persons we work for see their changes as growth rather than as a series of defeats or surrenders. When we negotiate with persons on something they do that bothers us, we are showing ordinary respect. When we unilaterally formulate a "treatment plan" to deal with it, we are showing an essential disregard for their thoughts and sensibilities.

Currently, everyone from actresses to physicians to "television personalities," all of them rife with insight and good intentions, seem to have published a diet and exercise book. None of them seems to have used Ayllon's approach (1963) even though it proved effective for the unnamed woman he used it on. The problems behavioral literature addresses tend not to be the same as the ones seen on the *Times* best-seller list. Journal articles address "management" issues, usually around food, clothing, bodily functions (that is, soiling and urinary incontinence). Has it never occurred to anyone to ask why these problems occur with persons who are labelled "retarded"? Why is there no literature for ordinary adults on food hoarding or dieting that use these same approaches? It is almost as if persons, once they are labelled retarded, become part of a different species that not only acts oddly but whose unusual activities demand unusual "treatment." Does getting *any* label necessarily make others and their problems so alien?

The answer is obvious. These problems are the only ones most persons labelled retarded are allowed to have. If they are living in impoverished environments where all they can actually touch is themselves, clothing, some simple furniture, or others, then it can hardly surprise us that a person will use available materials for expression. Have you ever read an article about "behavioral programs" for persons labelled retarded who like to get drunk and run up their phone bills with late night long-distance calls? Or how some persons labelled retarded have made themselves obnoxious with any of the sloppy idiosyncrasies of ordinary living? Of course not. The problems we read about sometimes appear rather extreme but only because such persons are not given the opportunity to be irritating in more reasonable ways. After placing our brothers and sisters in such bizarre environments with such minimal expectations, some professionals then turn around and react with indignation when confronted with bizarre responses. As Foxx* states:

---

*Foxx, R.M. "The use of overcorrection to eliminate the public disrobing (stripping) of retarded women." *Behavior Research and Therapy*, 1976, 14, 53–61. Reprinted with permission of Pergamon Press.

Public disrobing or stripping is one of the most disconcerting inappropriate types of behavior of the institutionalized retarded. The sight of a nude adult swaying from side to side in a corner, standing on a lawn or sitting in a chair masturbating openly can generate high levels of emotional behavior from various casual observers be they residents, administrators or visitors. The sensibilities of even experienced ward staff can be and are sometimes staggered by such sights. Public disrobing is not only socially unacceptable but may present a health hazard on poorly heated wards, especially for asthmatic residents. Stripping is a major problem in institutions for the retarded and one that is rarely treated.

There have been two common institutional approaches to the problem of stripping. The most common practise has been simply to cloister strippers from public view by housing them on locked wards and often within specific areas on the ward. The unstated administrative policy is that strippers should not be permitted to walk around the hospital grounds or taken on field trips outside the institution. This practise leaves the problem untreated and merely confines it to a specific location where the stripping can be tolerated. The stripper is often regarded as a "pitiful creature who does not know any better" and is left undressed. Occasionally a compassionate caretaker may redress the resident but, in general the resident is excluded from most social interactions and all training and educational efforts. The second approach has been to dress the stripper in clothing that cannot be removed. This use of restrictive clothing presents several problems. The residents' [sic] self-toileting efforts are prevented as well as toilet training efforts and toileting in general. In her attempts to remove the tightly fastened garments the stripper may begin tearing her clothing thereby adding a new inappropriate behavior to her repertoire. Neither of the above approaches are [sic] satisfactory or therapeutic. (p. 53)

Foxx cites a number of behavioral studies that have addressed disrobing. Hamilton, Stephens, and Allen (1967) used a 30-minute time out procedure "to eliminate the stripping of a retarded female in less than three weeks." Paul and Miller (1971) "eliminated the public disrobing of a 12-year-old retarded girl during 15-min training sessions within 20 sessions. . .with a 3-minute period in a time out room that followed each instance of stripping." Thompson and Grabowski (1972) reinforced remaining clothed. Schaefer and Martin (1969) reinforced remaining clothed with a "response cost procedure for undressing": since the woman was a heavy smoker, they contrived for an attendant to stand beside the woman and "destroy three of her cigarettes for each item of clothing she had removed. After 3 days the woman had quit stripping." But Foxx notes:

> Despite the success of the above programs, there are instances when the use of time-out and/or reinforcement for remaining clothed have not been effective in reducing or eliminating stripping. Even in instances where time-out has been used successfully its continued use has sometimes been prohibited by administrative edict. (p.54)

As an alternative to these procedures, Foxx cites his previous work (Foxx and Azrin 1972, 1973a, 1973b; Foxx and Martin 1975) as supporting an overcorrection technique.

> Briefly stated, the general rationale of Overcorrection is to educate the misbehaver to accept responsibility for his/her inappropriate behavior through the use of Overcorrectional Restitution procedures that require him/her to restore the disturbed situation to a vastly improved state. A second component, Overcorrectional Positive Practice, requires the misbehaver to practice appropriate responses in the situations where the inappropriate behavior occurred. Thus Overcorrection serves as an educative punishment procedure. The present studies evaluated an Overcorrection procedure that had been designed to treat stripping behavior. (Foxx 1976, p. 54)

In Study I, Foxx describes Amy, a woman whose record showed the "high frequency and durability of her public disrobing." She is reported as never having been included in off-ward activities since her "stripping episodes" were regarded as "completely unpredictable." It is hard to see how they thought this if her episodes of disrobing never occurred when she was away from the ward. Because Amy has a chronic asthmatic condition, she is "extremely vulnerable" to chills. "Also, staff felt that much of their valuable time each day was spent redressing Amy." Nonetheless, several "abortive attempts" to control this problem included using 10-minute time out after each stripping episode,

> requiring her to redress herself, positive reinforcement [not described] for remaining clothed, and placing her in a mesh restraining bag that restricted her arm movements while permitting her to walk. The restraining bag had been effective in preventing stripping but was discontinued because Amy, although toilet trained, had begun soiling herself since she was unable to lower and raise her panties. (pp. 54–55)

To get baseline data, Amy was observed for three days. If she were found nude, she was given a verbal reprimand and escorted to a time-out area for 30 minutes. "Except for the reprimand, all instructions were delivered in neutral tones and with as little affect as possible." After these three days of observation, an overcorrection program was begun, requiring Amy to wear extra clothing and assist in improving the appearance of other residents and their clothing.

> Whenever Amy was discovered nude, she was admonished, required to pick up her discarded clothing and escorted immediately to the ward clothing room where she was given Restitutional Overcorrection training in dressing. Amy was required to dress herself in the following items: panties, bra, slip, panty hose, her discarded dress, and tie shoes; her normal clothing was only a dress and occasionally panties and slippers. Graduated Guidance (Azrin and Foxx, 1974; Foxx and Azrin, 1972; 1973c) was given whenever Amy failed to imitate or complete the trainer's dressing instructions. The trainer would manually guide Amy's hands with his hands until she began the desired movements at which point he merely "shadowed" her hands with his. This shadowing action permitted the trainer to reapply immediate guidance when necessary. (p. 55)

While disrobing is not quite the shock Foxx makes it out to be, neither is it a socially generalizable skill. So the issue is not *whether* it would be more useful for Amy to change her way of acting than it is *how*. Would it not be more instructive for everyone involved to work with Amy in a way that would avoid a struggle? This program has the potential for Amy's refusing to comply. Foxx describes her as "a robust 190-lb, 52-yr-old profoundly retarded female." If Amy decided to protest this program to the point where she sat nude on the floor and refused to rise, to continue the program as described it would be necessary to struggle with her physically. And if we decided the consistency of this program was worth this struggle, what would this program be saying to the other persons who lived with Amy as they watched? If we believe that modeling behavior is a powerful teaching tool, what is being modeled while we "shadow" Amy's hands?

As soon as she was dressed in clothing her "trainer" had chosen for her, Amy

> was guided rapidly thoughout the ward where she assisted other residents in improving their personal appearance. The improvement of the residents' personal appearance constituted Positive

Practice Overcorrection and required that Amy: (1) button or zip up any undone clothing, (2) straighten residents' rumpled or twisted clothing, (3) walk to the ward clothing room and secure shoes or slippers for any residents without footwear and to assist them in putting on the footwear and (4) comb tussled hair. Throughout the Overcorrection training, the trainer delivered all instructions in a neutral tone of voice. This neutral delivery of instructions was designed to minimize any social reinforcement that Amy might associate with having been addressed by a staff member. (p. 55)

Amy's response to the overcorrection program was to decrease the number of times she took off her clothes. When the baseline condition of a 30-minute time out was reestablished, she greatly increased the times she was undressed. This makes one wonder why Amy would want to go to time out and why the persons working with her would make her going to a room by herself contingent on taking off her clothes. As it turned out, Amy used this "time out" to masturbate. This provided a real bind since this "reinforcement" could not be interrupted without "violating the time-out rationale":

An individual in time-out is free to engage in an assortment of inappropriate activities that will not be interrupted or discouraged. If the environment outside the time-out area is highly reinforcing, time out should be effective. When the outside environment is impoverished, the time-out period may be reinforcing and therefore, ineffectual as an inhibitory procedure. (p. 59)

What this suggests is that time out will not work. It is ineffective in institutions because the environment outside the time-out area is usually not at all reinforcing. It *could* work in a "socially normal" environment except that no "socially normal environment" could use it and still be considered "socially normal."

Study II involved Sherry, "a 31-yr-old profoundly retarded female with an assessed IQ of 12. . . . She was a stripper. . . . To control her stripping the ward treatment staff frequently placed her in physical restraint [*which*] consisted of placing a mesh restraining bag over her upper torso that tied at the shoulders and between the legs. . . . Sherry's stripping behavior forced her omission from activities that could have been reinforcing." (p. 57) If she could remain clothed for 30 minutes, she would be taken out for a 30-minute walk. Otherwise, if she took off her clothes, she was given the same overcorrection procedure Amy was. As Foxx reports:

The women's behavior when they were permitted outside the ward presented a curious paradox. The women had never been permitted off the ward because they were strippers. Yet when allowed off the ward they remained clad. Even before the Overcorrection training had eliminated stripping, neither woman removed her clothing outside the ward. Why were the women reluctant to disrobe outside? The most plausible explanation is that there were more reinforcing and potentially reinforcing stimuli outside than inside the ward. Not only were more reinforcers available outside, but they were changing constantly in magnitude, frequency and density in contrast to the too often sterile ward environment where reinforcement was infrequent and static. The constant availability and variety of reinforcers outside may have produced a natural programming of many behaviors incompatible with stripping. Also, the women may have learned in the past that whenever they publically [sic] disrobed, they were returned immediately to the ward i.e., timed-out from the outside world. Two ways of incorporating the above explanation into a ward program would be to program more outside activities for residents and increase the number of appropriate reinforcing activities on the ward. Implementation of these suggestions would increase the density of reinforcement which has been shown to increase the effectiveness of inhibitory procedures (Vukelich and Hake 1971). (p. 60)

If indeed the women were known never to disrobe when off the ward, why was getting off the ward contingent on remaining clothed? Couldn't Amy and Sherry, if they had been undressed simply been asked if they did not want to get dressed and go out? Still, the overcorrection procedure is assessed by Foxx as a "more humane and realistic way of treating stripping than other methods. . . . The stripper was treated not as an offender to be tied or locked up but rather as a person who needed more training in dressing skills." (p. 59)

It is important to understand, though, the historical context in which these approaches were developed. The degraded treatment that so many persons labelled retarded received—and still often do receive—in institutions is the background to this work. When behaviorists such as Foxx or Azrin began working with persons who were so radically devalued, they were at the vanguard for thinking that change was even possible. Their demonstrations of this ability to learn and to grow helped those who came later to see that not only was change possible but it was imperative. Their showing how readily persons labelled retarded could respond to the environment helped foster the idea that institutional environments are ultimately a disservice to persons with special needs.

The point of considering these articles is not to berate their authors for their work. Rather, it is to show that, based on what they have demonstrated, more can be done to improve the quality of life for the persons we work with. Unfortunately, though, much of this literature is not seen as an important breakthough for change but rather as a technology we can use to maintain an unacceptable status quo.

Because behaviorism is so good at looking at single behaviors, we can sometimes lose sight of the contexts in which these behaviors occur. I do not think of Amy and Sherry as suffering from training needs in dressing skills. Rather, I see them as needing a place to live in which the dressing skills they already had would be valuable. How one dresses (or does not dress) on a locked ward seems not to matter so much as it does for persons who do not live on locked wards. The circular logic that behaviorism is founded on (something reinforces behavior if it causes a behavior to increase, and we know it is reinforcing because behavior increases when we use it) can become the circular and punishing logic of a system that says, "We know you keep your clothes on when you're off this ward so we won't let you off this ward until you can keep your clothes on."

Why not approach these women and say, "We notice you sometimes take your clothes off when most others leave theirs on. Do you think a chance to learn more about dressing and grooming would help you feel more comfortable wearing clothes?" Then any number of realistic and positive steps could be taken in this direction, with the idea that eventually these women would stop publicly disrobing for the same reasons most other persons do not undress in public: no one else is doing it, and there is no reason to be the one to start it.

I think there are more plausible explanations for the way these two women chose to act. If, as Foxx's article implies, masturbation on the open ward was discouraged, then one logical place where Amy could get the opportunity for it was in the time-out area. If the persons working with her responded to Amy's disrobing by taking her to time-out, then she might well have interpreted the system to mean: if you want to masturbate, take off your clothes. It further seems probable that walking off the ward was sufficiently unusual to make it worth her postponing taking off her clothes until she got back to the ward. Or she may well have been sophisticated enough to realize that one did not masturbate in public.

These are only possible interpretations of these women's actions. Without the opportunity to know them, it is difficult to know what their actions meant to them. But by taking time to find out these meanings, we could negotiate with them to find alternatives. Just because persons insist on doing something does not mean they can never change. But if we could work *with* these women to learn what they wanted, then maybe we would have been put in the happy position of helping them get it appropriately rather than in the unusual position of forcing them to stop wanting it altogether.

—4—

Strategies of Behavior

If our goal for persons labelled retarded is the opportunity for an ordinary life, then we can begin to reach it by extending ordinary considerations. This sounds both simple to do and worth doing, but it has been an elusive goal. My experience has been that because of their labels—more than because of their specific or demonstrated needs—persons labelled retarded have been given things to do and places to live that are normal only for persons labelled retarded. Would anyone else find such a life acceptable?

Many persons today apparently think that living in a group home and working in a sheltered workshop is "community placement." But who—other than those persons we have labelled—actually works or lives in these places? What we have done in effect is to put little institutions rather than persons into the community. These group homes and workshops usually appear less forbidding than the sprawling and often remote "training schools," but they too efficiently segregate using the old rationale of "separate but equal." This means that the persons we work for often live not the way we do, but in a way we consider to be the "appropriate" equivalent of our own lives. This allows us to tolerate and even to expect the differences between the ways "we" live and the ways "they" live. Persons who work, for example, in the group homes are often former employees of institutions, and many times they have taken the same attitudes, approaches, and assumptions into "the community" that they used in the institutions. Group homes, for example, often have (or try very hard to get) a "time-out" room, which makes them much more like institutions than like any other home in the neighborhood.

It is the attempt at making life "normal" that requires, I think, the greatest reconsideration of behavioral approaches. There is little point in debating whether behavioral techniques work. Clearly they do. What needs to be considered is what they work for.

The model of behavioral intervention commonly used in these settings is the laboratory and the laboratory animal. Obviously, for reasons of research, keeping things isolated and simple makes an experiment easier to conduct and its results easier to believe. The challenge for behaviorism is to introduce these empirical findings into ordinary and nonempirical life in a way that does not require or recreate the laboratory model. I have worked with a number of programs that require an almost mechanical sameness of response whenever a person shows the "target behavior." This sort of routinizing of daily life can deaden spontaneity, creativity, and even sensitivity to our own situations. In working with *anyone*, do we really want a person to feel like a pigeon? And do we really need to feel like experimental scientists?

In doing psychological research with human subjects, the above feelings are sometimes inevitable. But all ethical research using human subjects requires their constant consent. Any person in a study who gets uncomfortable is free to leave. But in agreeing to participate in someone's research project, there is an unavoidable element of feeling "acted upon" rather than "acting." One might be asked to perform certain tasks or answer certain questions without a clear understanding of why all this is happening. For those with a sense of cooperation and humor, these experiments can be mildly amusing or mildly boring. But how do we carry what psychologists have learned from these experiments into practical life? We do not, I hope, need to continue the same atmosphere of surveillance and mystery inherent in research.

This is an old charge against behaviorism—that it is "cold" and "unfeeling"—it is also an unnecessary one. There is no reason we cannot pay attention both to research and to social realities. In working with persons labelled retarded, for example, we can use task analysis to make what is complex simpler. But my experience is that many persons using behavioral interventions reduce complex social situations too simply. For example, "attention" is thought to be a powerful reinforcer, and for many persons it is. But it is too simple to think that "staff attention" will universally maintain a "behavior." Similarly, I think it unlikely that "ignoring" (that is, withholding attention, especially "staff attention") will work any more effectively when used routinely. I have seen many "behavior plans" that automatically use these two social devices as a carrot and stick. But these are used as if the persons they were being used upon are motivated very differently from the ways we are.

The persons we work with are much more like us than otherwise. Think of some chore around your own house that you do not much like. Suppose you can cope with house chores except for making the bed, doing the laundry, or shopping for groceries— something basically trivial but eventually unavoidable. Do you think you would do it more often if others around you automatically said, "Good bed making, Karen!" Or do you think you would stop some minor annoying habit if others in your life ignored you? Would you really want to come back for dinner if everyone at the table pointedly stopped talking to you and refused eye contact every time you scraped your plate or mispronounced "erudite"?

So how *do* we negotiate the minor irritations of life? I can have at least a little patience with someone who leaves the cap off the toothpaste because I know I have the irritating habit of leaving coffee cups around the house. I can understand someone not doing the grocery shopping because I hate making beds. In other words, I can see my own shortcomings in others and tolerate their imperfections in exchange for their tolerating mine. But I have a very different attitude when I think these irritations are not from careless inattention but are intentional. If someone forgets to meet me for lunch, I can understand—we all make embarrassing mistakes like that on occasion. But if I am stood up three times in a row, I begin to make certain inferences about the other person. I may react with irritation that this person cannot say, "I'd rather not have lunch with you," or I may be angry at being systematically inconvenienced. In any case, I have gone beyond the actual behavior and started asking, "Why is this going on?" The conclusions I draw—accurate or not—will help shape the way I respond to the situation.

I think most persons work this way. But many times I have seen "behavior plans" that ignore these social conventions. It might well be that I do not like doing dishes and I let them stack up before getting to them. But if doing dishes is my chore in a group home, I will not have the option of doing them when I want to. Often the chore must be done within a specified time limit, or else I will be labelled "noncompliant." If this becomes an issue between me and the persons working in the home, then it is likely to be referred to a "behavior specialist" who then develops a plan to "help" me with this problem. This immediately starts on the wrong foot: why is something that irritates *all* of the persons involved *my* problem?

This sort of reduction immediately starts what I see as an erroneous chain of reasoning. If it is *my* problem, then *I* am responsible for fixing it. But in fact it is *our* problem and, for convenience, we blame one person who has a part in it. Because behavioral thinking is skilled at breaking the complex into simple units, I think it can break the person apart from his or her social life and community without noticing it has done so.

The way behavioral thinking has been misused, though, often gives credit to the persons doing direct service and blame to the person ostensibly served. For example, behavioral science explains quite efficiently why I will wash the dishes after dinner every night if, when I do it, someone tells me how much I am appreciated. Obviously, I am reinforced by this attention, and it is the "staff attention" that keeps me on task. The problem comes when I do not do the dishes. Is it assumed that the persons working with me are somehow deficient in finding some valuable reinforcement for me? This is not usually the case. My experience is that I will be considered "noncompliant" or "unmotivated," and something will be done *to me* to correct this problem.

One thing that might be done to me would be to set up a behavioral plan so that when I do the dishes I will get a reward, but if I let the dishes pile up, I will not be rewarded. This seems like a "positive" plan until you think of how it might feel. If I do not do the dishes at all, I will never earn the reward. A plan like this is less likely to work since I will not miss what I have never had. So a way has to be devised to let me know if I did do the dishes, I could get something pleasant. Perhaps each evening for dessert I could be given a hot fudge sundae. Then, after several nights, I would be told, "Tonight's hot fudge sundae will be ready for you as soon as you have done the dishes." Theoretically, it would be my "choice" whether to earn the reward or not. But think of how this actually feels. Is it any different from your being told that you will get a raise and then after a week being told, "Since you got your raise, we've decided to give you more work. If you don't want to do more work, then you can get your old salary, or you can work harder and keep your raise. It's your choice." Is there any way you (or your union) would be able to interpret this plan as "positive"?

In fact, there might be. An event in and of itself has little meaning without understanding the social setting it takes place in. What we often need for our own understanding is a reason *why* someone does something. For example, I will indeed work harder for less money if I think a cause is worthwhile. But why I think it is worthwhile is an internal process.

A simple example might be helpful. Someone steps on my foot, speaks, and I shrug. Or someone steps on my foot, speaks, and I shove that person. Obviously, the behaviors are the same, but my response to what was done has been quite different. One reason is my understanding of the person's motivation. If someone accidentally steps on my foot and I see it as an ordinary, unavoidable event, then I have an inclination to forget about it. But if every time we meet, this person purposely stomps my foot and says "Gotcha!" I am more inclined to be irritated. My experience has been that few behaviorists will argue this and would, on the contrary, say, "It is this sort of consideration that has to be done before a behavioral plan can hope to be effective." The problem is that this sort of consideration is frequently abbreviated for persons labelled retarded.

That an organism will respond to pleasure as a motivation more readily than to pain is a starting point, but what is needed is to know *why*. This is not all that compelling when we are dealing with "organisms," but it is too rich a speculation to ignore in dealing with persons. Our best guess as to what others intend is how they present themselves. As every poet, lover, politician, and soap seller knows, *what* you say is not as important as *how* you say it. In using behavioral plans we often try to achieve a good end and appear to be unfriendly. Is it possible that we could be more convincing to those we serve if we tried achieving a good end in a friendly way?

* * *

Most of us speak more clearly with what we do than with what we say. One common problem in daily life is trying to understand what other persons mean when they do something. This is often a complicated process even when we can talk things over with them. But often the persons we work with cannot say in so many words what they mean, and when we try to understand their motives in doing something, we are forced to guess. So when we work with persons who cannot express themselves clearly except through the way they act, we are always guessing what those actions mean and what ways will help them express themselves more effectively.

Some guesses are better than others. If we assume that Dean sometimes spits at others because "all retarded people do obnoxious things like that" or because "he's a spoiled brat," then we are making no progress in helping Dean with his spitting, much less his understanding of himself. As a rule, most of us are more interested in getting something than in defining ourselves. So Dean is more likely to spit as a way of keeping those who frighten him away than he is in getting the label "spoiled brat."

Rudolf Dreikurs, an Adlerian psychiatrist, thought that "misbehaviors" help discouraged persons feel a sense of community. If they did not feel valued, then they might resort to one of a few basic strategies—seeking attention, power, revenge, or displaying inadequacy—to get that feeling of being useful and needed, the feeling of belonging.* Dreikurs assumed that all persons want a sense of individual dignity within the community at large. Using this as a starting point, we will consider these goals as helping better to explain some common situations.

Strategy I: Attention

> Every afternoon, John Robert gets back from his training program to the state "school" he lives in just as the first shift meets with the second shift. He goes to his room to change into casual clothes for the afternoon; then he goes to the door outside the meeting room and begins to demand to see someone to talk to. When he is told that everyone is in a meeting and that the person he wants to see will be available in ten minutes, John Robert throws himself onto the floor. Sometimes he will take off his clothes. At other times, he has taken a piece of broken glass so he can threaten to slice his wrists. At this point, someone leaves the meeting to calm John Robert.

In considering this situation, my first question is "How is this behavior adaptive for John Robert? What is he after, and why does he think this is the most efficient—or the only—way to get it?" Un-

---

*An enjoyable and concisely well-written explanation of these strategies appears in Dinkmeyer & McKay's *Systematic Training for Effective Parenting (Parent's Handbook)* (1976). Dreikurs conceptualized attention, power, revenge, and displayed inadequacy as *goals*. I have modified them here as *strategies*. My own assumption has been that if most persons are working for individual dignity and community acceptance, then these four routes are strategic in attaining the goals of acceptance and accomplishment.

fortunately, in working with some persons, the answer I often get is "He only does this for attention" as if wanting to be noticed were a mysterious or stupid need. It is obvious that we all act in ways we hope will get us attention, especially "positive attention." But the need for recognition is so great that if positive attention is not available we will settle for negative attention.

In general, others make inept and unpleasant bids to be noticed because they lack confidence. They fear that if they do not make dramatic efforts to be noticed, they will be ignored. Many persons decide it is better to be spoken ill of than not to be spoken of at all. If this is true, then saying a person does something "only" for attention really does not tell us much about how we can change it. But if we think persons engage in some activities because it is the only way they can get attention, then we can best help by teaching them more sophisticated ways of confronting and satisfying a basic social need.

Persons with difficulty in expressing their wishes, thoughts, and feelings have fewer ways of controlling the environment they live in. This in turn leaves them with even fewer ways to manage themselves comfortably. If I have too difficult a time at work, I can quit. If I do not have another job to go to and I feel I have to work in a place I do not like, I can take some steps to make my life more tolerable, even if all I can do is complain with my coworkers during our coffee break. Often people will express discomfort by acting it out only because there is no other way to express it. When we dismiss these messages as demands for attention that do not deserve our notice, we are denying these persons the only way they know how to change their lives for the better.

Sometimes, the way that people act is a cry for help; sometimes it shows the need for reassurance, for affection, or for just a simple demonstration that they are valued by those around them. Because of our different backgrounds, we all have different ways of expressing these simple needs. If I know that all I have to do is say, "I feel discouraged" to get someone to help cheer me up, I will say, "I feel discouraged" when I want to be cheered up. But if I cannot say those words and if, when I want to convey my sense of defeat, I am ignored, then I will feel not only discouragement but possibly rage or complete defeat. I might move to another strategy: something frightening or violent.

It is useful to ask first how and why frightening others helps make life easier for John Robert. I tend to think that the way others make us feel is the best indicator as to how they themselves are feeling. When two people get married, they often have a party to share their happiness. When others are going through a difficult time, it is not surprising that we think of them as being grouchy or worse. So when John Robert does something that is irritating or frightening, my assumption is that he himself feels angry and afraid.

John Robert had many strengths. He could speak clearly and articulately about what he was thinking and feeling. He had been able to maintain his job outside of the institution, and he had already lived in several community homes. Each of these moves ended when he had become anxious, threatened to kill himself, and was taken to a more secure institution. Once he was readmitted, though, he would regain control and become angry that he had to live with "retarded people." Feeling superior to the persons living with him, he also felt above "house rules." For example, John Robert would leave without letting anyone know. Because he had often threatened suicide, most of the persons working with him felt more comfortable knowing where he was.

This resulted in a constant struggle. Because he saw himself as "better" than the persons he lived with, John Robert would demand special attention. He considered only the persons who worked with him to be his social equals, and if they did not give him preferential treatment, he would threaten to run away and kill himself. To prevent him from doing this, they ended up having a person work with him exclusively. This cycle of his asking for attention, being refused, and then successfully blackmailing others for it had developed gradually. John Robert apparently did not consciously plot this, and it was only after some time that the persons working with him became aware of what was going on. Before they realized the predictability—and efficiency—of this system, they were only aware that John Robert was "a problem" and that they did not like working with him. When they talked about him, they described him as "spoiled," "nasty," a "brat."

Once it was understood that the way John Robert and they were working together was not spontaneous "nastiness" on his part, they started interpreting his threats of self-injury as a way of gaining social contact. The mistake they had been making was in seeing this need—rather than his method of satisfying it—as unreasonable.

Everyone in this system, including John Robert of course, felt as if they were in a bind. Those who paid attention to him felt as if they were being blackmailed by his threats and were "rewarding" him for them with their company. On the other hand, John

Robert did not feel that they would notice him at all unless he threatened something they could not ignore. As he understood it, others were saying, "The only way we will pay attention to you is if you threaten to harm yourself." So they were actively encouraging him in the one thing they wanted him to avoid. Of all the persons in this system, John Robert was the least able to break the pattern; so a plan was developed to give him better options in getting consistent and positive attention.

The positive part of the plan was to engage John Robert as much as possible in casual social situations. If others were running an errand and they wanted company, they were encouraged to ask him along. If they were doing anything they thought they would enjoy having John Robert join them in, they were encouraged to include him.

This did not mean that he was to be their friend. They were to be friendly and talk to him about how he might make friends on his own, which he could do in community social groups he went to. He was reminded that the persons working with him could be friendly, but their roles were different from friends. I would mention in passing that it is often difficult to make this distinction in working with others. When we work closely and intensely with someone and if we basically like him as well, the relationship often feels the same as a friendship. But there are real differences. We are not paid for the time we spend with our friends. If we quit our jobs, it would not disrupt our present friendships. The same cannot be said about our relationships with the persons we work for. So long as we are in some sense made to feel responsible for a person, it is difficult to be on the equal footing of a friendship. Of course if we should stop working with someone and go on to develop a friendship with him or her later, then that is a different matter.

The point of this plan was to let John Robert know that he could spend time with others without having to make threats. It also let him know that relationships are formed by mutual convenience. Some people, then, would be seeking him out more than others, because some of them would find him more enjoyable to be with than others. This approach was to give him a chance to learn how ordinary relationships work.

This approach takes time, but time is a key part of it. "Negative behavior" rarely fails to get immediate attention. As a result, it can easily produce immediate reinforcement. Earning positive attention with positive social strategies is a riskier procedure:

not every positive social action gets a positive response. But in the long run, positive relationships can be a more valuable, though less dependable, source of attention.

My friend Dr. Jordan Markson often makes this point by asking which you would rather do: earn $500 by getting the first ten persons who walk down the street to hate you or by getting the first ten passersby to love you. To get the $500 you have to persuade all ten to have the same reaction to you. Obviously, few choose to try getting the first ten persons to love them because a positive response is subject to too many variables, while there is a large repertoire of approaches one can use to guarantee a negative reaction. Being frightening has the virtue of being dependable: others will almost always react and in the same ways.

With any challenging problem we face, we ask ourselves what can be changed. Since John Robert's needs are so great that he is willing to use extremes to satisfy them, we cannot realistically expect to change him either directly or immediately. But if we have little "control" over John Robert, we have a good deal over his environment. We have many more options if we try to offer him the opportunity for change by making some differences in his daily living. Specifically, if he needs attention, even at the price of being potentially self-destructive, then our goal would be to provide the attention he needs as much as possible in a way that is more socially agreeable. And if he could rely on the goodwill of others in return for this, then his world would be more predictably pleasant, and the predictability of being unpleasant would be less necessary.

If he could trust others to spend time with him without his having to make threats, then John Robert would not need to frighten others so much. And if his threats also caused less excitement, then their effectiveness would diminish even more quickly. To make these bids for attention less exciting for everyone, a time was set aside for John Robert to make dramatic announcements. Since he seemed to enjoy doing this, it would simply be provided safely, rather than taken away.

Each day, when he returned from work, one person was to go to his room and ask him if he needed to threaten himself. Since the others working would be at their meeting, one person would be specifically designated to hear his threats and *whatever else* he might want to say. He would be given the use of a room with plastic instead of glass windows and with nothing but a sofa in it. This way he could throw himself onto the sofa or bang the windows without harming himself. When this idea was first discussed, some thought it would "reinforce" John Robert's threats and acting out.

They were further irritated to give him exclusive one-to-one attention during "their" meeting. But the point of this was that if they
planned to ignore John Robert's requests for attention, then he already had the ability to force them to give him one-to-one assistance. Rather than leaving this situation in John Robert's control, this plan would help them feel more cooperative while at the
same time helping John Robert feel in charge.

The persons using this approach first practiced with one another so that when it was presented to John Robert, he would see
it as being a sincere effort to help him rather than to mock him.
The plan was presented, approved, and monitored by the Human
Rights Committee as another step to help insure that this would
be a genuinely helpful—and not sarcastic—approach to John
Robert's needs. Some interpreted this plan as paradoxical. In a
sense it is, but with an important difference. With paradoxical instruction, persons are told to do something (such as make threats)
with the idea that they will refuse to comply. This often takes on
the appearance of a game. Our approach was not a game but a
different way of acting socially. This approach was designed to take
cues from John Robert himself and, as honestly as possible, give
him the opportunity to get what he wanted without engaging in
struggle. By offering him the opportunity to make his threats,
others were able to give him the message: "We don't understand
necessarily why this helps you, but if you think it does, then let's
do it in a way that is not frightening or hurtful."

In presenting this plan to John Robert, it was made clear to
him that making threats was not required and that if he wanted
to talk about other things, that was okay. He agreed to try this, and
when his time to make threats arrived he found that he did not
need to make them. What he apparently had wanted (we had
guessed correctly) was the guarantee of some time to talk. The
time was for him to use as he saw best. The point of this intervention was to emphasize that others would pay attention to him
regardless of how he acted; so he could choose the way he thought
best to act with them. When asked if he wanted to act out in any
way, John Robert could then hear himself say, "I don't have to do
that" rather than hearing others say it for him. The change that
this approach brought was to show John Robert he was responsible for his actions and their "consequences" more than anyone
else could be or wanted to be.

The second part of this was to explain to John Robert that his
safety could not be guaranteed if he were to pose a serious risk of
injuring himself. Since it was impossible to tell a serious threat

from a casual one, all of his threats would be taken seriously. The one exception of course would be in his scheduled time where his threats were to be taken as something he needed to say at that moment and not necessarily expressing serious intent. But if he should get angry or frustrated and spontaneously threaten to harm himself, he would be taken to the crisis unit of the local mental health center.

After this part of the plan was explained to John Robert and he had agreed to it, he did indeed threaten himself with a piece of glass and was taken immediately to the health center as a psychiatric emergency. As soon as he got there, he broke a window and repeated his plans to kill himself. The providers told John Robert that they did not have the facilities to admit suicidal or dangerous persons and that he would have to be taken to a psychiatric hospital. John Robert had previously been admitted to this hospital and chose not to return.

After this episode, his threats stopped. He changed to the point where he decided to try a move to a group home. He had some initial difficulties in adjustment, but these had been anticipated, and he was able to maintain sufficient control as not to return to the state "school."

* * *

Ed did his work well except for the times during the day when he would call out to others. He articulated words with difficulty; so it took extra effort to understand him. Others, already busy with their own work, could not always make time to listen to him as quickly as he wanted them to. As a result, they would say, "I'm busy right now. Can we talk about it at break?" Ed would sometimes forget to talk about what had been bothering him at break and would remember what he had to say once everyone was back at work. This frustrated him and made the persons working with him feel hardhearted for denying him the time he needed when he needed it.

As this situation went on, he apparently decided that he was not being given a fair hearing, and he became persistent in his demands. "Hurry," he would say, "it's real important." Some found that "real important" could mean he wanted to tell someone he did not like them anymore. Some persons began to get the feeling that Ed was demanding this time "just to get attention."

Some of his supervisors had started to respond to this "problem" by telling Ed that his interruptions bothered them. To help him remember not to interrupt or be unnecessarily demanding, they would remind him the first two times he interrupted that he could speak to them at break. But with the third interruption, he would lose the "food reward" that he could have otherwise have been given at the end of the day. The persons who developed this plan saw it as "positive reinforcement" because the reward was presented for "desirable behavior" (not interrupting) and not for "undesirable behavior" (interrupting). From Ed's perspective, though, it was punishment: sit down and shut up, or we will take away your reward.*

The real problem was not that the persons who developed this program misunderstood what they were doing. They could call a program anything they wanted: its effectiveness would not depend on its name. The problem with this approach was what it "said." It said, "You annoy us and we will make you pay. Continue to do it, and it will cost you food."

Would it not be easier and kinder for everyone to give someone like Ed what he really wants and to do it in a way that leaves the persons helping him feeling helpful rather than punitive?

The first step is to try to understand how these interruptions help Ed. It is not hard to come up with some probable ideas. When he demanded attention by telling others to hurry over and listen to his important message, he had learned that the only legitimate way to engage others was to feign an emergency. Naturally, no one will ignore a call to hear something "important" since many things legitimately demand immediate attention. Just as naturally, though, others became irritated with his "crying wolf."

This was awkward for everyone. Ed's articulation was not improved by the pressure of having to say quickly what bothered him. He knew that, once his "emergency" was found not to be a

---

*This "treatment plan" illustrates one of the problems with current use of behavioral principles: the ideas are easily grasped, but the systems in which they are used are not. Reinforcement, by definition, increases a behavior, while punishment decreases it. I have found it commonly assumed that, if a person is given a reinforcement for *not* doing something, this plan is considered a positive reinforcement plan. But reinforcing "noninterrrupting behavior" is really a cover for punishing interruption. Just because Ed could earn food for being compliant does not make the plan positive—compliant is much less easily defined than the real focus of the plan: annoying interruptions.

critical one, the persons he had called would move on; so he had to articulate something dramatic and this further removed him from opportunities for ordinary conversation.

The challenge was to give Ed the chance to speak calmly and without pressure about ordinary concerns without his having to make them dramatic in order to be listened to. Since it was impractical to try to provide that spontaneously during work time, it was decided that one person would meet Ed as soon as he came to work in the morning. The persons who worked with him told Ed that his interruptions suggested to them that having someone to talk to was important for him (as indeed, it is for everyone). Since it was hard to be able to do that during the workday, could he plan to spend as much time as he needed when he arrived in the morning? Ed called this his "very important meeting."

At first, Ed took about 15 minutes to describe his concerns. The person listening checked with him before ending each session to make sure he had said all that he needed to say. If during the day, he needed to interrupt someone's activity, he was reminded that he should remember to bring it to his meeting the next morning. Since these meetings were scheduled, he developed the habit of remembering what he had to say. And since he was not hurried in them, he was able to relax and speak as clearly as he could.

After three months Ed was making fewer interruptions at work. He began to take about five minutes for his meetings and seemed not to need them every day. Reassured that if he had something to say others would still listen, he sometimes would say, "I don't need to meet this morning." Of course, if during the day he had something to say without interrupting, others were willing to listen: this approach was concerned only in helping Ed not to irritate or disrupt others. It did not attempt to isolate to one part of the day a time for him to speak. And because Ed did not need to demand attention in unreasonable ways, others felt they could offer it to him freely. The end result of this approach was that Ed and the persons who worked with him had reached the give-and-take used in ordinary conversations.

* * *

George Smith's mother has had cancer for the last three years and has been taken to the hospital for the fourth time in three weeks. George lives in a state "school," and his mother used to pick him up every weekend, but when his mother is in the hospital, George does not get to see her as much as he used to. He has been told at various times that his mother is getting better; at other times that she is getting worse. This uncertainty, almost from day to day, has been emotionally draining on George. At times during work, he will interrupt work by saying, "I wish you were my sister" or "What if your last name were Smith, too?" Even before his mother's illness, George has said things like this to others, but now this has increased. The previous plan was just to acknowledge that he had been heard and redirect him to his work. Now those working with him would like to revise this to reflect his current needs for reassurance.

It would be easy to think every bid for "attention" would somehow be obnoxious. This is, of course, not so. Anyone in George's position can appreciate his concerns: his mildly unorthodox way of expressing himself is easy to forgive under the circumstances. Would anyone want to use a "behavioral plan" in this case? Would anyone want to ignore him? Would someone really like to reward him for every hour, say, he did not ask for reassurance? Or if he did say something "out of turn," would they recommend withholding the reward? Is this situation George's problem? Or is it the problem that he feels the need for reassurance more than he feels reassured?

The persons working with George decided they did not need a "plan." Instead, whenever he made one of his unorthodox remarks, the person he was speaking to would let him know they understood that this must be a rough time for him and ask him about how things were going. Of course, if he mentioned his mother, they would say what they felt was most comforting, such as their hoping that his mother would get well; that things would work out for the best. Sometimes, they suggested that he call the hospital, talk to his mother or the nurses there and hear firsthand how things were.

As I have said, we sometimes interpret understandable needs merely as ploys for "attention." Maybe this is sometimes the case. We can all understand George's plight. But is *anybody's* need for "attention" beyond our ability or willingness to understand?

* * *

The plans above have involved certain assumptions:

A person will continue a "negative behavior" because—however unlikely this first appears—it is somehow adaptive. Our first task is to learn the answers to the questions, "How is this adaptive?"

Persons usually do things to get some beneficial result—not to get themselves labelled. If a person constantly seeks attention, he is probably not looking for the label of "spoiled" or "manipulative" so much as a way of getting some needs fulfilled.

The way that others behave make us feel is probably the best clue to understanding how they themselves are feeling.

The need for attention is a given. What is negotiable is how a person chooses to get it.

Positive attention is harder to win than negative, but a person will choose to get negative attention rather than be ignored. The challenge is to help others understand that while positive social relationships are less predictable they are, over time, more rewarding than negative relationships are.

Most persons tend to act the way they are expected to act.

It is best not to ignore dramatic bids for attention. Ignoring only encourages a person to become more dramatic. It is better voluntarily to give attention to a person sooner than be forced into giving it later.

Scheduling an opportunity for "inappropriate" or maladaptive strategies for attention can make them less irritating for everyone involved. By removing the element of surprise, a person is given the opportunity to learn cooperation more calmly.

When others have the opportunity to do something inappropriate or irritating on a regular basis, they also have the opportunity to say, "I don't have to do that." This gives them the experience of deciding *for themselves* what they need and having that decision taken seriously.

The way a person acts should produce as natural a result as possible. Saying to a person, "When you threaten to hurt yourself with broken glass, we will have to get you help for this problem" is a more natural consequence than saying, "If you don't stop doing this, we will punish you with restraint or medication or loss of privileges."

When we pay attention to what a person does, we are not necessarily "reinforcing that behavior." We are opening the opportunity for a dialogue with the person. When we ask, "What does this mean for you?" we are making the first step to answering the question, "How can we help?" The second step is to say, "If you need help with something, here is another way to ask for it." This message can be trusted only if we have demonstrated that we are worthy of trust.

Strategy II: Power

> Each evening in a residential unit of a state institution for persons labelled retarded, the persons who live there are told when to take their showers. When John tells Audrey it is time for her shower, she tells him she will not take it. When he tells her that she has to, she sits on the floor and cries. When John gets two women to help him, they pick Audrey up as best they can and drag her to the bathroom. There they undress her and struggle until she is under the water and at least partially washed. Often, after this is finished, Audrey stays up part of the night yelling that they cannot push her around. Sometimes, she quiets down and goes to sleep; other times, she continues to yell until she is physically taken to the time-out room. If she continues to remain noisy, the nurse is called for emergency medication to quiet her.

Another strategy is power. In order to feel we have it, we often imitate powerful persons. This is seen in ordinary life so often that we hardly notice it for what it really is. When John Kennedy, a young, handsome, powerful person who did not wear hats was elected president, hat sales in the United States dropped immediately. The reason, one assumes, was not that Kennedy intended to punish persons wearing hats. A more likely hypothesis would be that the persons who stopped wearing hats felt somehow improved by imitating the president. Certainly, people see power in different ways. Some persons think of political figures as powerful; others think of entertainers, sports figures, or persons they know in their daily lives. Most of us consciously believe that we buy products for the values they have. But when some admirable person endorses a product, it has no real effect on its intrinsic worth, but sales go up anyway.

Persons living in institutions often imitate persons who have the power to make decisions. This is probably as true in universities, the military, and other institutions as it is in state facilities for mental health or retardation. It is not at all surprising that we find the persons living in these institutions imitating the persons who work there. Unfortunately, when they do so, they are often misunderstood. Instead of being flattered, some persons misunderstand and take offense. For example, persons who work in these institutions often decide when "their residents" will take showers. Realizing this, some persons try to take showers when they decide rather than when they are told to.

For example, when Audrey was told it was time to shower, she would lie on the floor and refuse to get up. If someone tried to pick her up, she struggled. Sometimes, one or two fully clothed persons had wrestled her into the shower and forcibly washed her. One wonders what could have happened to lead to a struggle of these heroic proportions for so little consequence.

As I have said, the way others make us feel is the best clue as to the way they themselves are feeling. If this is true, then both sides of this struggle acted as if they felt powerless. So giving both sides the opportunity to cooperate would give them less need to assert themselves with displays of power.

It is not difficult to see how persons can feel powerless living in an institution where they are told when to get up, when to eat, where they will work, when to shower, and when to go to bed. But persons working in direct service themselves often feel unappreciated and powerless in their jobs. Often they have the least flexibility in determining their hours and their duties and the most accountability to their supervisors for what actually happens in the course of a day. Because of this, they often feel far less autonomy than they actually have. They sometimes forget that they appear far more powerful than they might themselves feel. As a result, when they think someone is challenging the little authority they see themselves as having, a struggle ensues.

Power is the strength to be self-determining. That is, the more I can do about my own life, the more powerful I will feel. Similarly, when persons we are working with feel powerless, one approach to that problem is to give them more responsibilities. Audrey's problem was not, as it turned out, taking showers. She had no argument against feeling clean. It was against being told to take showers.

The commonsense solution then was simply to ask her. Since the persons working with Audrey felt they had to coordinate the showers within a certain time, they did not have an unlimited range for her to choose from, but being given any choice at all was what was expected to be effective. This would be even more effective if the reasoning behind the choice is also obvious. Arbitrarily picking two times would not be so effective as two options based on the limits of the actual situation. This is also an opportunity to share these considerations with the other persons Audrey lives with so that each person gets to choose a good time for herself. So, when she was asked, "Audrey, which is a better time for you to shower—at 7 or 7:30?" Audrey (to their surprise) quickly agreed to 7. At 7:20 Audrey was showered and calmly watching television.

Suppose, however, that Audrey did not want to choose either 7 or 7:30 for her shower. Suppose she said 8:30, and when the time came she refused. At this point, it would be easier to think of this as an expression of her need for attention, that if she did not do this, she would risk being ignored. One approach then would be to find ways of engaging Audrey socially and thereby giving her another avenue of relating to others.

Or Audrey might be bored, as is often the case in institutional living. Forcing others to drag her to the showers might be highly entertaining. In any event, others could respond by saying, "Well, Audrey, it's your choice. We can't make you shower." In situations similar to this, my experience has been that Audrey will just quietly take a shower on her own, and nothing further need be said about it. I have yet to use this approach with the result that the person refused ever again to shower.

But suppose Audrey decided to wait everyone out. The fact of the matter is that Audrey does not live in a vaccum. We all need to cooperate with one another to live in any society; so eventually Audrey will need someone's cooperation. If her not showering has made her unpleasant to be near, then others would be able to say, quite naturally, that she is asking for cooperation she is unprepared to give, that her not taking a shower has made it difficult to be with her. If she continues to insist that she does not want to shower, others can again explain to her they cannot force her to, but neither can she force their cooperation. This makes sense only if she sees this as the natural result of her own choices and not as a punishment arbitrarily inflicted on her.

This approach gives Audrey the dignity of risk. If, for some reason, I decided not to bathe for a long time, others would probably take notice and eventually someone would ask me when I planned to wash next. If I failed to take seriously the discomfort I was causing then I could hardly expect them to look forward to being with me. (Although, not bathing for extended periods of time is an effective method of getting others to go out of their way for you.)

In a sense, the persons working with Audrey had always been giving her choices to make. The problem was they had presented her with options they did not really want to offer her. When we ask a person, "Do you want to do this?" we should be prepared to be told, "No!" Sometimes, "no" is not a realistic answer. If a person with diabetes needs to take insulin, we are only inviting a problem to ask, "Do you want to take your medication?" The question is more effectively presented as, "Is this a good time for you to take your medication?" If the answer is "no," then we can ask, "When will be a good time for you?" If the person is noncommittal about this, it would be fair to suggest a specific time. This makes it more difficult to engage in a struggle and respects a person's sense of autonomy.

Often the apparent struggle is a part of a larger, less obvious, conflict. Few persons are willing to fight over taking or not taking a shower, but many are willing to do almost anything to preserve their sense of self-esteem. Giving options provides the opportunity to cooperate rather than the feeling of being coerced.

Giving persons the natural consequences of choices they have made seems like common sense. But some persons have difficulty in understanding what this means. For example, if persons refuse life-supporting medication, it is not really in their best interests to respect their choice since the natural consequence is that they will die, an experience from which they will learn nothing useful for their future with us.

But if a person refuses to take a shower, what are the "natural consequences"? Some persons say, "If you can't take a shower, then naturally you can't watch TV or listen to your radio or do anything except go to bed." I strenuously object to this. For one thing, it is incongruous to really associate something as refreshing as sleep with punishment. And it is absurd to think that persons who are not freshly showered cannot see a television screen or hear a radio. Instead of saying, "I am punishing you for noncompliance with my wishes," we sometimes pretend our reaction is a "natural consequence." Often the person being punished sees this as the arbitrary choice it really is.

It is far more effective to let the "consequences" of refusing to take a shower be realistically natural ones. If a person's refusal to do something is a matter of convenience, then, as I have pointed out, she loses other persons wanting to cooperate with her—not their cooperation necessarily, just their willingness to. If she chooses not to bathe for an extended period of time, she runs the risk of being avoided by those who object to the resulting odor. In other words, what would happen to Audrey for not showering is what would happen to any of us. Anything beyond this is inflicting punishment, and Audrey will see it this way. Sometimes the choices that persons make are punishing for them, and that literally cannot be helped. What can be helped is *our* punishing others.

This example might seem extreme—how could anyone get into a struggle over showering? Except all this actually happened. Unfortunately, this illustrates a standard problem: it is not hard to find examples anywhere, from among our own circle of friends to international policy, of those whose underlying assumption is: "I feel comfortable only when I am in charge of a situation." Such persons can unnecessarily provoke us into asserting our own authority. Or if they are greatly more powerful than we are, we feel we have to give in to them. In either case, power is made to seem important. It does not matter if I fight a person to assert my own authority or if I surrender: both strategies make power the basis for our common social strategy.

The best way to avoid power struggles is to live cooperatively. One way to do this is to redirect our attention from a challenging area to a neutral one where we can find a common ground. For example, Jane likes to help others she thinks are falling behind by assembling their work for them. In one way, this is a thoughtful thing to do, but of course others cannot learn to do something if someone else is always doing it for them. If someone suggests that Jane do only her own work, she gets irritated. Sometimes she will return to her work and appear to sulk; other times, she will begin shouting that she is not appreciated and noisily storm from the workshop.

Part of this problem is the way this situation is interpreted. If we see Jane as a busybody who needs to have limits set on her, then we will approach her differently from the way we will act if we see what she is doing as a warm desire to help others. One of the major points of this book is that most persons tend to act as they are expected to. If we treat Jane as if she were already acting cooperatively, then she is more likely to try to live up to that expectation by acting more cooperatively in the future. So rather than confront her with our irritation, it is better to interpret what she is doing in a way closest to how we wish she were acting. For example:

> Roger has just been working all morning on packaging and has managed to get 30 done. This is a real achievement for him since he has often had difficulty in attending to task. Jane, though, has done 180. She feels she has done enough for herself and is now helping Roger. When Linda, their supervisor, walks by, she feels that Jane is interrupting Roger's progress.
>
> Linda: Roger, you've done more of these this morning than you've ever done before. You must be really proud of yourself having paid attention like that. Jane, did you notice how well Roger was able to work on his own?
>
> Jane: Yes, I did.
>
> Linda: And Jane, you've done all the work you started with. You must have been really busy.
>
> Jane: I was.
>
> Linda: Well, which would you rather do? Get more work for

yourself or help me in the kitchen getting ready for break?
    Jane: I'll help you in the kitchen.

As you can see, a number of points were made in a very short time:

Roger's accomplishment was publicly noted.
The way Linda complimented Roger helped promote the idea that he is in charge of how he acts, and that is a source of satisfaction for him as well as for others.
Jane was redirected from interfering with Roger's progress in a way that left her feeling helpful.
Jane and Linda avoided a power struggle because Linda interpreted Jane's actions as "wanting to be helpful" rather than "bossy" and offered her the chance to be helpful in a way that really was helpful, that is, sharing kitchen chores.
Jane also gets to expand the number of things she can do with this method of redirecting by substitution.

This example seems too easy. The point of it is to show one way to avoid making simple challenges into confrontations. But what could be an effective approach if Jane insists on helping Roger even when redirected? What if being Roger's "supervisor" is the only role in which she is content to work?

This approach does not claim to prevent all problems all of the time. One major emphasis of this way of working with others is that we take our cues from them. If Jane were to insist on being Roger's supervisor, we would have to negotiate with her about what that means to her. Is it her way of being friendly with him? Does she really want a social relationship with him, and is being a "boss" the only way she knows? Does she feel deprived of status in her life, and does being his "boss" compensate for this? For purposes of this particular example, these speculations focus primarily on Jane. But in the more complex reality of daily life, we would want to consult with Roger about his thoughts and feelings on all of this as well.

Situations can appear to be generic, such as being power struggles, but be very different in specifics. We cannot, alas, expect a simple formula to handle all of them. But there are some simple, basic ideas and attitudes that can be helpful. One commonsense starting point is for Jane to make certain that when she talks about these challenges, she makes sure it is a good time for the others, too. Better to negotiate with Jane in a scheduled, unhurried, and friendly meeting than right at the moment she is trying to tell Roger what to do.

More can be accomplished when we check our interpretations of events out with one another. No one is threatened (or threatening) by saying, to Jane, "When you do Roger's work, I get confused. I don't understand if you are trying to be his friend or if you are bored or what?" This gives Jane room to explain how her actions might have understandable motives that could be satisfied in more appropriate ways.

Persons who need power in order to feel as if they belong often show this need slowly. Gradually, they demand more and more, and only gradually do others begin to resist so that after weeks or months or even years everyone involved begins to feel locked in a struggle. The approaches discussed here are ways to avoid such situations. But if they do develop, these approaches are also ways of reshaping conflicts so that both sides can feel more comfortable in cooperating than they do in competing.

This example clarifies how this can be done with persons who can explain their needs to us in words. But if persons cannot articulate their needs clearly, then we can use this same approach, but we would use their *actions* as their response rather than their words. For example, Gregory never told us why he needed to throw his work. But when we told him our best guesses as to why and offered the best assistance we could to help, we were in effect negotiating a solution to the problems he was experiencing.

Some persons I have worked with have told me, "What you are really saying is let the client win once in a while"—which is not what I am saying at all. What does it matter who "wins" if the other person has the feeling of having "lost"? If the goal is to cooperate rather than to compete, then everyone needs to reach some form of agreement. Only with competition can there be winners or losers. In a genuinely cooperative system, the terms win and lose become irrelevant.

One of the basic premises of this work is that we all need to work with others *as persons.* To do this, we need to see anyone we work with as eligible for the same rights, considerations, and life we ordinarily expect for ourselves. It is difficult to maintain the concept of "us" "winning" over "them" and still see "them" as our equals. This sort of team mentality is somewhat excusable in high school football competition but not in many other places. Even in war, which one used to be able to win or lose, has become a situation where there are no winners and only losers. I think that is the end point of any competition system, that when winning becomes the goal, the process becomes so cutthroat as to make the competition useless or counterproductive.

Major Points Relating to Power

Persons seen as powerful have greater status and are more likely to be imitated. Persons who have a limited exposure to the ordinary range of powerful models in society will use the limited ones they know. Persons living in an institution will imitate those they understand to be powerful. Since one definition of power is the ability to decide for oneself, this sometimes leads to struggles when persons have decisions made for them.

Power is inappropriately modeled when it is used to force. When we force someone to "cooperate," we are really announcing that power is the most important asset for being socially effective.

Cooperation is a good model to show how we can take one another's needs into consideration while at the same time taking care of our own.

Persons who feel powerless can be helped to achieve status by using the skills they have to help others.

Strategy III: Displayed Inadequacy

Beth has lived most of her life in state "training schools" before she was recently transferred to a nursing home "in the community." She is at least 20 years younger than the next oldest person living in the home. The persons who work there are reluctant to place demands on her and tend to treat her as a child. At the same time, she has begun a training program for vocational and daily living skills. Before beginning this program, Beth had never gone shopping or made her own lunch. Beth sometimes presents a challenge when she is given the chance to try something new because the first time a new task is presented she typically pushes it aside and puts her head down on the table, refusing to look at it.

I had been asked to help at this program in developing "behavior plans," but because there have been so few "serious problems" and so many areas for social growth, I decided to spend the time in weekly groups. I saw these groups as a transitional stage where persons could practice assertion skills and discuss their problems and concerns with someone outside the program. My goal was that everyone in this program would eventually be able to talk freely about a problem without unnecessary anxiety.

Everyone seemed to find these groups enjoyable except for Beth, who refused to come to the first meeting. When she came to the second meeting (after a week's encouragement to do so), she pulled her chair from the circle, turned it to face the wall, spoke to no one, and refused to respond when spoken to.

Those who work with a person like Beth often ask, "How can I motivate her to participate?" or even just "How can I motivate her?" These questions are usually well intentioned. Still, they provide a poor starting point because it starts a line of speculation that ends no better than it began. How could someone motivate you—or anyone—to do something? The most effective method, in the short run at least, is through using force. Bank tellers are occasionally motivated to hand over large sums of money because the person asking for it has a gun aimed at them. So we could "motivate" Beth, in the short run, by forcing her to do the things we want done, but as soon as we decide to stop this coercion, she will probably be even less eager to cooperate with us than before.

This question of how we can "motivate" a person involves some unpleasant assumptions that those who ask it usually do not share. It presumes that we know the lives of others better than they themselves do. Sometimes this can be true. We all have made mistakes that our friends could have told us to avoid, and we all can see self-defeating things that others persist in doing, even when they acknowledge that these things are troubling. But when we try to "motivate" someone to change to our way of seeing things, then we are assuming that we have the right to insist upon that change, to get other persons to live their lives as we think best rather than how they think best. Is this something we really want to do?

As mentioned earlier, Rudolf Dreikurs thought that one strategy for persons who present challenges was to display inadequacy and that this represented the last stage of discouragement for an individual. Not only do such persons feel inadequate to meet life's demands; they also make those around them feel inadequate as well. What often happens to such persons is that they are nagged until they get angry. Those around them learn that it is easier to avoid them than to end up struggling with them. Since being alone feels "safer" for such persons, it eventually becomes their chief ambition. If being alone represents safety, then the challenge is to find an area of strength and use it to give a person an increased sense of competence and security.

Each week, Beth came to the group. At first, she was encouraged to go with no expectation other than her being there.

Sometimes this worked and she would come to the room where we met and then sit with her face to the wall. Some weeks, though, even this minimal expectation was too much, and she would refuse to come. But, eventually, over the next couple of months, she began coming to the group more regularly, even though she did not participate.

When I began that particular group, I was surprised to learn that even though some of the group members had been working together for years they did not know each other's names. So I began structuring the beginning of each meeting with activities such as learning how to make introductions. Regardless of what we did, I always gave Beth the option of joining in. Initially, she would make no response that she had even heard, later she would react by pulling her chair further from the group, and finally she would shake her head "no" whenever spoken to.

Her next change was to come to the group even if she had not been given several reminders. She would sometimes mutter comments at the wall about what we were talking about. These remarks grew louder, and she gradually turned her chair at an angle so that she could turn to the group or the wall, whichever she felt she needed more. Sometimes her muttered remarks were funny, and when we all laughed she would give a little smile as if she had accomplished something, which, of course, she had. Gradually, as she became confident that she could be effective in this new format, she began talking in the group in the same way that others did, although some weeks she had more to say than others.

At no point did her talking or not talking become an issue. When she spoke, we responded; when she declined to join in, I would say something to the effect that Beth apparently did not feel she needed to join in with the group that day. My point in doing this was to avoid personalizing her anxiety about speaking. I wanted her to feel that she could talk when she chose to, rather than doing it to please others.

I do not want to give the false impression that I was naturally relaxed during this process. It took energy for me to restrain myself from actively encouraging Beth more than I did. It was difficult to remember and actually carry out the fact that the best I could do was to provide a safe and friendly environment and hope that Beth would grow to trust it over time. For many weeks, she decided she wanted nothing to do with this group, and I would feel in some way responsible: if I were a better group facilitator, she would be a better group member. Fortunately, I was able for the most part to check my own needs and frustrations in this and gave her time and room to grow.

Persons who are as discouraged as Beth often take very tentative first steps. Beth's first steps were to try to show the group that while she would be there physically she would not join in. Her first comments to the wall suggested that she thought little of the group members or of me, and she would imitate what someone had said with a nasty accuracy that sometimes stung. But if she did this, I would ask, "Did something I say upset you, Beth?" In this way, I could impress upon her that whatever she chose to say would be taken seriously.

The point of this discussion is that we cannot "motivate" a person. Persons "motivate" themselves. What we can do, though, is provide an atmosphere of trust and support so that as a discouraged person gradually works at developing confidence we can help justify that sense of accomplishment. This can be frustrating at times. Often such persons can make us feel as discouraged as they themselves feel, but with a little patience and ingenuity, the resolution of this situation can be rewarding for everyone involved.

After a year and a half of meeting weekly with very few interruptions, Beth gradually came to see the group as a real resource for herself. As is often the case, this program was changed radically when budget policies were revised by the state. Accordingly, the groups were going to break up. As a result, we spent much of our last meetings talking about what we had experienced and what we expected to experience. On the very last day, Beth came to the group meeting visibly upset. "I have to tell the group something," she said. "Pat made fun of me this morning and I am upset." Pat had not meant anything of the sort and these two—who had begun by not knowing each other's names—then proceeded to settle this misunderstanding on their own and ended with handshakes and hugs.

Rhonda is a 24-year-old woman who has serious visual impairment and is partially paralyzed. She has recently moved to a new "dormitory" at a state training school and at the same time begun to work in a different training program nearby. Persons working with her previously used a "behavior plan" that said, in its entirety:

Behavior Plan

1. When Rhonda holds her hand up near her body, she is doing this for attention.
2. Ignore this.

This gave some hint as to how Rhonda had been understood.

The persons working with Rhonda in her training program noted that she had difficulty in finding her work area and that even with daily reminders for the past month she still would not walk even in the right direction when she was getting ready to begin working. Some days she was able to demonstrate good work abilities, while on other days she would appear not to be able to. They wondered if this were not "passive aggressive behavior." She usually did not want to go to gym, and once there she would throw a bean bag or basketball in such a way as to suggest she was angry. What should be done about this? Finally, whenever she was asked to do something, even if she later decided to do it, she would say "no." Some were taking her "no" seriously and trying to persuade her to say "yes."

When persons have physical disabilities, it is difficult to find a fine line between setting one's expectations too low or being unreasonably demanding. After discussing this, we decided that perhaps because of her physical challenges it was easier for Rhonda to be reminded where her work station was than it was for her to find it on her own. The approach was to find a way of making her finding it important enough to her to do it herself.

One way we found of doing this was to give her greater autonomy. This was done by not taking her saying "no" literally. Because of her physical involvement, it was felt that her spoken "no" could mean "yes." Rather than take her verbal response literally, we decided to ask her if she wanted to do something and then leave it there for her. If she said "no" but then did it anyway, we could then say, "Oh. I guess you meant 'yes,' Rhonda." That way she could get the message that improving her speaking abilities could be useful for her. This in turn gave her the opportunity to see why she might want to work, but did not make work more of an issue than what she wanted to make of it herself. In other words, we could use what she did as her language rather than what she said. This gave her the choice of doing what she wanted without having to say it.

Since I assume most persons enjoy doing what they do well better than what they do poorly, I could understand why a person with paralysis might avoid vigorous gross motor activity. By giving her the option of just sitting in the gym or doing what she liked, the gym became a more positive place for her, and her reluctance to go diminished. She still showed some effort in throwing things, but that was to be expected.

After several months of this, Rhonda no longer had as much trouble finding her place at work.

Virginia sometimes seems to be confused. When it is time for a break, she will just sit at her work station and not move. If she is reminded that she can go, she will start to but then just stand there. Others assume that she does not want to join in and are content to leave it at that, except that Virginia has been known to move swiftly through lockers taking food and money. At first, when it was time for a group meeting, Virginia would show up late or not at all. Now that she has made friends with others in the group, she comes more regularly. But when it is her turn to speak, she needs several prompts before doing so. The persons working with her see the challenge as getting her to cooperate without "reinforcing" this repertoire.

This is an interesting situation in that Virginia is apparently using all three strategies we discussed simultaneously: she is using her displays of inadequacy to draw attention for herself in her group, and she is using it during the break to exert power over others by taking their possessions. The response here, though, might well be the same as it is in any situation: to develop a rapport with her so that she feels more status in being part of the group than, as is the case now, she does being outside the group.

Jim, the director of Virginia's training program, felt that he and Virginia had a reasonable understanding of one another; so he decided to talk with her about this. He pointed out that he disliked nagging her to join the group, but at the same time he really looked forward to seeing her at the group meetings. Could they agree that, rather than his reminding and coaxing her all the time, he would remind her once, and she would do the best she could with that? Virginia agreed.

At the next group meeting, Jim told Virginia that her turn was next. When it was her turn, she stood up but did not speak. Jim waited her out. She apparently felt awkward standing there and finally spoke. Since her refusal to participate did not give her any special role or status, she started speaking without demanding reminders. Others remarked on the change, and this helped make life more enjoyable for Virginia as well as for the persons she worked with.

By asking her to help out during the break, she was given a greater sense of responsibility, which kept her busy and away from the possessions of others. Whether it was this increase in status or the decrease in opportunity, Virginia's stealing dropped. In any event, her need for attention was used to "buy out" her need to display inadequacy. Similarly, her sense of personal autonomy went up, and her need to use these maladaptive strategies to feel a sense of power went down.

* * *

Many training programs use a type of behavioral plan with work cards or charts to note a person's success for a specific target behavior such as "works cooperatively." Often, such persons keep their cards with them so that if they succeed or fail in a given area then a note can be made on the card. At the end of the day, with a certain number of successes, they get to choose a reward, typically food. These programs usually have different levels. The level of persons with the most training needs, for example, usually get the most opportunities for rewards. As they become more skilled, though, it is thought they do not need as many rewards to "motivate" them; so the number of times they get rewarded is cut down. Often, using this system, as persons acquire more skills, they started to become "unmotivated."

Sometimes apparent displays of inadequacy are unwittingly fostered by our own efforts to help. In this case, the "lack of motivation" had been unintentionally made part of a program. The reward for "doing better" was to be paid less. Even beyond the logical error this program makes, I think it makes a more serious social error.

Using the expectations of others as a tool to shape someone's behavior is risky. It might be relatively benign for a brief time, but most persons work with many different expectations over the years. Each new person has a different set of expectations as to what constitutes "good behavior." With each new and necessarily different "behavior plan," we give different variations on the same theme: "I know best—so shut up and listen." No actual plan says this, but I think this is the cumulative message these plans send.

The question here is, of course, what do we want to "motivate" these persons to do. In this case, the goal was for persons to be "motivated" for work.

I assume environment to be powerful in shaping how anyone acts. So the challenge was not to devise a new scheme that would get these trainees to fall in line. The challenge was to find ways of making the environment expect more of them than it did. For example, this group could plan on going out together once a week the way many persons who work together do. Many places use going to MacDonald's as a reward for complying with a "behavior contract," but I think this is a poor plan. Instead of making it contingent, it should just be made available. If we assume a person will learn how to act in public best by actually being in public, then the persons with the most challenges need experience with public events the most. Making these experiences contingent on how a person acts in more restrictive, institutional, or private settings guarantees that the persons who need them the most get them the least.

In talking about planning regular and noncontingent community experience, the persons in direct service cite not having enough time or persons as one obstacle. "We have Karl who needs someone to help him with his wheelchair, and we have Richard who wanders off.... That means we need two staff members already." In other words, the persons in direct service were displaying a sense of inadequacy. Is their display any different from the ones they want to "treat" with "behavioral programs"? Is their sense of inadequacy, except for their abilities to express it, any less frustrating for them than the discouragement other persons experience for themselves?

Rather than developing a "treatment plan for the staff," we worked to recognize the creative options already available. For example, why not help Richard with his wandering by having him help Karl? We already had good reasons for avoiding community exposure in large, easily identifiable groups since these only called further attention to the differences of the group members. Would it not be better for everyone if only two persons, one trainer and one trainee, went at a time? That way they could really get to spend the time talking and learning rather than in managing and feeling managed. By thinking creatively, we were able to develop positive options that turned this "impossible situation" into something enjoyable for everyone involved.

When we think of "motivation" for the persons we work for, we are sometimes tempted to think of them as having completely different ways of working with the world than we do. Certainly, I do not propose that everyone everywhere is alike. On the other hand, I find it hard to believe that any group living within a given culture is capable of being so different as to constitute another species. So the needs for "attention," "power," and, if all else has disappointed us, the need to display a sense of defeat are ways to understand the persons we work for. These possibilities are just as likely to help us understand ourselves.

There are no individual solutions for systemic problems: by focusing only on the individual's specific problem, we lose the person. By focusing on the individual alone, we lose this person's social definition. Unless we consider the complete social system a person lives and works in, who can we help?

Strategy IV: Revenge

> Betsy did not like the breakfast cereal at her group home. Rather
> than indicating this or eating something else, she threw all the
> cereal away, which made the others feel angry. When Betsy was
> given a job she did not like in the workshop, she threw some of
> the materials into the dumpster. When the job could not be com-
> pleted without these materials, all the members of the workshop
> were inconvenienced and irritated.
>
> Howard's friends were paying a great deal of attention to
> Patty's new canvas tote bag. At lunch Howard's friends were sur-
> prised to discover that their lunches were gone from their usual
> places and more surprised to find them in the trash. Howard later
> admitted having thrown the lunches away and explained having
> done so by saying that he was tired of hearing about Patty's new
> tote bag.

Rudolf Dreikurs thought that revenge was another stage of a
person's discouragement. Sometimes these expressions of that
sense of defeat can feel like a power struggle, but the difference is
that power struggles leave both sides feeling the need to gain control of the situation. A person who resorts to revenge feels hurt and
wants to retaliate. Betsy's relationship with the persons she lives
and works with is generally a good one. When she throws things
away, others feel confused and hurt, as if she had done it against
them personally. Similarly, Howard's throwing his friends' lunches
into the trash left them feeling confused and hurt and wanting to
get even with him.

If we ask how this is adaptive for Betsy and Howard, the first
thing that comes to mind is the swift effectiveness of their messages. In both cases, it is clear how Betsy and Howard feel. It is
clear and effective because with just a few gestures they have left
others feeling the same way. The temptation, of course, is to produce stern consequences and show Betsy and Howard that "we
don't tolerate this sort of behavior." Of course, in doing so, we only
justify their assumptions: that others neither listen nor care. If they
see their actions as their best attempts at communication and
these efforts are met with retribution, then it only furthers the idea
that socially ordinary ways of communicating are ineffectual.

One useful intervention for persons who feel the need for revenge is to teach them how to be appropriately assertive. This can
be done regardless of the person's present level of expressive skill.
If persons can speak, then we can help them identify the feelings
they have about different situations and express them. This is dif-

ficult for many persons in our culture; so this training could well be an opportunity for everyone involved to learn better assertiveness skills. I have been training persons in these skills for over 8 years, and I wish that with all of my exposure to such training I could claim complete and constant command of these skills for myself. But the point is not that we can train others never to feel frustrated. What we can do is to show alternatives to feeling *hopelessly* frustrated. So when I lose my temper, I do not have to feel that was the only response I could have made; I can feel instead that it was one of many I could have used.

Persons who can speak can learn to say, "I don't like the cereal we have here." If they are answered with, "Tough luck—eat it or starve," then we can see a justification for their discouragement. But if the reply is, "Which cereal do you like?" then we are beginning a dialogue. This response begins changes toward leaving everyone more comfortable.

But suppose Betsy or Howard cannot speak. In this example, both Betsy and Howard have demonstrated that they can express themselves and that their actions are their best communication. A person with the motor skills to do what they did can also learn some simple signs. If nothing else, they might be able to sign thumbs down for things they do not like. If we respect their displeasure, then they will be more likely to express it in this more ordinary way than with the sorts of things that irritate and anger others.

Once again, our task is to provide an alternative for an unpleasant or irritating situation. I am assuming that the behavior of others is their best way of letting us know how they feel and that they let us know this by making us feel the same things that they feel. So our job is not always to address our feelings in return, but to help them learn new and more effective ways of expressing themselves. If we take a person's inability to communicate effectively as discouraging, then we help remove some of the discouragement by giving the person an effective way of communicating. Once this discouragement is helped, then the person is more free to express feelings other than those of defeat.

Major Points Relating to Revenge

Persons who make us feel angry and hurt are expressing their own anger and hurt. If we respond with the sort of punishment we would find emotionally satisfying, then we are only continuing a cycle of frustration and pain.

By isolating people's expression of their feelings, that is, by focusing on their "behavior," we neglect the social system in which
the behavior takes place. Accordingly, we could eliminate a
particular recurring example of something irritating that a person does, but we will not have satisfied the person's original
wish.

This approach assumes that all persons appreciate the opportunity
for full membership in social groups that are important to
them. This does not mean that all persons want to belong as
active participants, but they do want the assurance that, if
they did want to join, they could.

Competence as a Motivation

> Maria was tightening the bracket on a glue dispenser she uses for
> her work when Arnold walked by. He said, "Put that screwdriver
> away, Maria, and get back to work." Maria shrugged and con-
> tinued working. "Maria," he said, "if you don't put that screw-
> driver away, I'll take it away from you." At this point, Maria, who
> has a hard time speaking clearly, threw the screwdriver down
> and walked away. A few minutes later, she returned and threw
> the money she had been paid for that day's work at Arnold and
> walked off again. Arnold thought she had gone to the toilet; so
> he did not follow her. A few minutes later, Maria threw a rock
> through a window by Arnold's desk. When Arnold went outside
> to her, she threatened to throw a rock at him. Finally, with the
> help of four others, Arnold was able to get Maria back to the work-
> shop and to "time out" so she could "cool down" and get back
> to work.

The day after her "acting out," the persons who worked with
Maria told me how she had been trying to dismantle her glue dispenser to "test" Arnold, who was new to the program. Rather than
let her "get away" with this, though, he had tried to set "reasonable limits," but the more limits he set, the more Maria acted out
until she had escalated "out of control."

Maria, too, was eager to explain what had happened. Since
English was not her first language, she spoke with an accent. More-
over, the fevers she had as an infant left her with somewhat slurred
speech. So whenever she got excited, her speech could be difficult
to understand. Thus, it was with some difficulty that Maria explained her version of what had happened.

She had been fixing a loose bracket on the glue dispenser

when Arnold told her to stop. She wanted to explain that she was fixing it *for* him. Because she was caught up in this repair and because it would be an effort to explain herself, she just kept working, thinking Arnold would see on his own how she was helping out. But the next time Arnold came by, he told her to stop or he would take the screwdriver away from her altogether. At this point, she felt frustrated by not having made the repairs quickly enough, at being misunderstood, and by being threatened rather than reasoned with. All of this felt confusing and frustrating to her. Since she felt incapable of explaining this to Arnold, she told me that she just left the building and started throwing rocks.

I knew Maria valued her ability to fix things. She enjoyed telling me a story about when she lived in a state training school. The ward stereo system was broken, and no one else could figure out what was wrong until Maria repaired it by checking the electrical connections by herself. It seemed that her pride in this sort of accomplishment was more important to her than almost anything else. Because of her difficulty in making herself easily understood, Maria's manual skills were a source of status for her in her community. Arnold had not yet learned this. If he had, he might have acted differently.

If, for example, he had simply *asked* Maria what she was doing rather than interpreting it himself, then he could have encouraged her to continue or even to have her show him how to fix the glue dispenser. One of the rewards of having learned something can be getting to teach others. Instead, by devaluing Maria's achievements, Arnold managed to discourage her. Maria's throwing rocks, a sort of revenge, demonstrates how alienated and discouraged she felt by his response. When she was taken to time out, this punishment further demonstrated to her how hopeless her situation was.

Once he found out that Maria had wanted to show him how well she was doing, Arnold felt as if he had undervalued not only her skill but also *her*. Just as he wanted to be able to show others some things he felt he could do well, he could understand Maria's wanting to. This need for accomplishment or growth, not just in work but in other areas as well, was one he felt he shared with Maria. Just as he felt that he had a lot to learn in his work—and how much he enjoyed sharing his gains in learning to do it well— so too could he see Maria doing the same with her work. This sort of understanding can be the basis of a relationship between us and the persons we work for. Arnold had seen Maria as someone he "trained." After this episode, he was able to see her better as someone he was in training with.

Thinking of achieving, maintaining, or demonstrating competence as a *motive* can put others in a positive light and can give some creative possibilities to pursue. Rather than looking at Maria as "noncompliant," we can see her instead as someone eager to do something well. Because she has shown that she enjoys displaying mastery, we can use the accomplishment she has shown as the basis for expanding her areas for competence. It would be a good start to recognize her abilities with repair work and use these as a foundation for the kind of work she does. Rather than have her do assembly or packaging work, we could negotiate with her for a training program to refine and expand the skills that she already values. For example, it could be that she would enjoy working on electronic equipment (such as stereos or radios) more than on mechanical equipment (such as washing machines or bicycles). Once she had chosen a type of repair she would enjoy most, then she could be trained in the skills needed for competitive employment in doing it.

* * *

One of the early interests in psychology was the problem of motivation. Robert White (1959) presents a concise history of motivation as well as a theoretical synthesis in the idea of competence.

> I have chosen the word *competence*. . . . [to] refer to an organism's capacity to interact effectively with its environment. . . . We need a different kind of motivational idea to account fully for the fact that man and the higher mammals develop a competence in dealing with the environment which they certainly do not have at birth and certainly do not arrive at simply through maturation. Such an idea, I believe, is essential for any biologically sound view of human nature.

For a long time, the idea of instincts and drives had dominated the discussion of what "caused" behavior. Freud (1949), for example, felt that instincts were the "ultimate cause of all activity." While he felt that there were an indeterminate number of instincts, at one point he speculated that they all derived from two basic ones: Eros and the "destructive instinct." This theory has never been proven "wrong" so much as other ideas have been able to offer a more economical explanation.

White (1959) summarizes drive theory:

Using hunger as the chief model, the orthodox conception of drive involves the following characteristics: (a) there is a tissue need or deficit external to the nervous system which acts upon that system as a strong persisting stimulus; (b) this promotes activity which is terminated by a consummatory response with consequent reduction of need; (c) the reduction of need brings about the learning which gradually shapes behavior into an economical pursuit of suitable goal objects. In this scheme the tension of an aroused drive is interpreted as unpleasant, at least in the sense that the animal acts in such a way as to lower the drive and becomes quiescent when it is lowered. There are probably no living champions of so simple an orthodoxy, yet the scheme remains pervasive.

White then considers some early experiments in motivation that involve neither instinct nor drive. For example, he cites Dashiell (1925) and Nissen (1930) for their observations of white rats crossing an electrified grid "simply for the privilege of exploring new territory." White (1959) notes how Hebb (1949)

has been particularly insistent in reminding us that many of our activities, such as reading detective stories, skin-diving, or driving cars at high speeds, give clear evidence of a need to raise the level of stimulation and excitement. Men and animals alike seem at times bent on increasing the impact of the environment and even on creating mild degrees of frustration and fear. Hebb and Thompson (1954) reflect upon this as follows:

"Such phenomena are, of course, well known in man: in the liking for dangerous sports or roller coasters, where fear is deliberately courted, and in the addiction to bridge or golf or solitaire, vices whose very existence depends upon the level of difficulty of the problems presented and an optimal level of frustration. Once more, when we find such attitudes toward fear and frustration in animals, we have a better basis for supposing that we are dealing with something fundamental if a man prefers skis to the less dangerous snowshoes, or when we observe an unashamed love of work (problem solving and frustration included) in the scientist, or in the businessman who cannot retire. Such behavior in man is usually accounted for as a search for prestige, but the animal data makes this untenable. It seems much more likely that solving problems and running mild risks are inherently rewarding, or, in more general terms, that the animal will always act so as to produce an optimal level of excitation. (Hebb & Thompson, 1954, p. 551)" (pp. 313–314)

This has far-reaching implications for the lives of persons with "special needs." Such persons are typically described as needing a "well-structured program," which translates into a predicatble (and often boring) routine. Ideally, "good structure" would provide each individual with enough predictability to maintain a sense of security but, at the same time, enough novelty and challenge to maintain an interest. This is related, of course, to what we usually think of as play. According to White (1959):

Being interested in the environment implies having some kind of satisfactory interaction with it. Several workers call attention to the possibility that satisfaction might lie in having an effect upon the environment, in dealing with it. Groos (1901), in his classical analysis of play, attached great importance to the child's "joy in being a cause," as shown in making a clatter, "hustling things about," and playing in puddles where large and dramatic effects can be produced. (pp. 315–316)

That a person's interest in the environment depends upon having a satisfactory relationship with it makes a provocative challenge. If the persons we work with have been taught limitations and have been discouraged or misunderstood, then if we are going to "motivate" a person we have to show that there is something satisfying available. Often the things we present for them to learn and to master mean more to us than to them. Learning to sort by color or mastering nuclear physics are meaningless accomplishments unless they have meaning for the person who has learned them.

A "satisfactory relationship with the environment" sounds very much like a nonbehavioral concept, since it seems to imply an internal "feeling" that behaviorism would consider irrelevant. But this concept is, in fact, central to behaviorism: White says "Skinner (1953)...describes it as 'operant' and...thus 'emphasizes the fact that the behavior *operates* upon the environment to generate consequences.'...A rat will show an increased tendency to press a bar when this act produces a click or a buzz." In other words, doing something can be "reinforcing" in and of itself. If it has an impact on the environment, it is even more "reinforcing."* (p. 316)

White (1960) notes an interesting event in child development:

> Around one year there is likely to occur what Levy (1955) calls "the battle of the spoon, the moment when the baby grabs the spoon from the mother's hand and tries to feed itself." From Gessell's (1943) painstaking description of the spoon's "hazardous journey" from the dish to mouth we can be sure that the child is not motivated by oral gratification. He gets more food letting mother do it, but by doing it himself he gets another kind of satisfaction—a feeling of efficiency and perhaps already a growth of the sense of competence. (p. 110)

This example was similarly difficult to explain with drive theories because if the child's motive in eating is hunger, the person who feeds the child is satisfying the hunger more efficiently than the child can. For the same reasons, the child is not being reinforced by the food. The behavioral hypothesis would be that the child is reinforced by this experience of being effective.

This then provides one avenue of approach: if mastering a challenging is in and of itself satisfying, then finding one meaningful experience of mastery for a person opens the door to others. There is, of course, evidence that the baby's apparent satisfaction with this experience of mastery is one that we keep well into adult life. This sense of mastery is a large part of humanistic psychology's "growth," and losing the delight of mastering challenges can be seen as a type of psychic death. One economical explanation for

---

*Considering this, one can see how effective behavioral techniques can be. For example, using time out is a powerful intervention since it deprives a person of opportunity to experience a stimulating, hence reinforcing, environment. Furthermore, in time out, there is little one can do to have any effect on the environment. Typically, such places as time out rooms have nothing in them. But my argument is not whether behavioral approaches are effective in shaping behavior—they demonstrably are. But what is necessary to consider is in what social context they are used. If we think of a novel environment as a rich source of learning, then, using behaviorism's preference for reward rather than punishment, we would try to place persons with serious learning needs in ever more rich and stimulating environments. Doing so, we would be trying to encourage learning new skills to address old challenges. When we use time out, though, we are punishing without presenting alternatives for change.

what we call play is the pleasure of competence. But for whatever historical reasons, we tend to think of things we do only for the sheer joy of being effective as being less valuable than the things we do to accomplish tangible results.

When President Kennedy announced the goal of landing a man on the moon, he was asked why we should commit our energies to such a project. He could do no better than to say, "Because it's there." One of the interesting phenomena to observe in our landing astronauts on the moon was the care NASA took to show how technology had benefited from this venture. While Alan Shepard sliced golf balls across lunar craters, scientists on earth pointed out the improved technology in medicine, computers, and other "practical" sciences. Somehow the triumph of successfully arriving in another world seemed frivolous unless it could also help our everyday earth-bound lives.

The feeling of doing something well is—apparently—in and of itself gratifying. This would seem to be the reason skiers wait in long lines to go skiing. Nothing tangible is achieved except the occasional broken bone. But one of the reasons skiing can be exhilarating is that it provides the feeling of achievement at having learned successfully to negotiate a challenging environment.

This sense of achievement, obviously, is strongest for the person doing it. But many of our "behavioral" approaches pretend this is not so. Many programs specify that after Karen successfully completes the targeted behavior (learning to discriminate by color, for example) she will be "reinforced" with "Good sorting, Karen!"* Do you think skiing would be more fun if we were given rewards of attention after every run? I do not. I think there is something intrinsically rewarding for us when we accomplish something valuable for ourselves. Often when we teach a skill, we praise the person we have trained for having learned it. That can be a mistake.

If I am teaching you how to drive a car and I say each time we finish, "I am so pleased with your progress," I am telling you that I am pleased, but I am also indirectly giving you a way to displease. All you have to do is drive badly. What am I going to say then?

---

*Again, if it increases behavior, we have to call it a reinforcement, but there is no need for us to assume that all reinforcements have equal value. "Verbal praise" is an effective reinforcer for some persons, but I am interested in getting as much mileage from an intervention as I can. Hence, my "verbal praise" tries to foster self-esteem and self-evaluation while at the same time acknowledging a success.

Similarly, when we work with others and say, "I am so happy you had a day without throwing anything," we are telling them, in a fairly direct way, that anytime they feel annoyed with us they can just throw something. This way of talking also condescends. Would you really want to learn to drive to please me? Do we really want the persons we work with not to throw things just to give us pleasure? Hardly. The real reason is that learning to drive and learning self-control are skills most valuable to the persons who have them.

I think it more efficient and honest to say, "You must be proud of how well you are doing," This encourages self-assessment. This leaves persons with more freedom to contemplate what they themselves have done and how it makes them feel rather than making them look at what they have done "for" us. If we really believe that feeling effective is rewarding, then we are being most helpful in teaching others to recognize the feeling of accomplishment in themselves.

This sort of approach is more global in scope and would aspire not to "treat" one behavior (such as "noncompliance") but coordinates persons' strengths so as to better help them to limit their weaknesses.

One challenge this book addresses is: How do we adapt what we have found in theory, under experimental conditions, to socially ordinary environments? By considering the desire to be effective as a motive and a reinforcer, we have found a useful tool. If we see the persons we work for as being challenged by their environments, then we can see the value of teaching mastery in something that is valuable to the individual we are working with. This assumes ordinary persons will learn more quickly if they see or feel a potential benefit from doing so. One way of teaching is not to focus on the skill itself but on the ways in which the skill can be used. Persons who have never seen snow will be confused by our attempts to teach skiing, just as persons who have never worked for a check, gone to a bank, or bought things for themselves at a store will be baffled by our attempts to teach money identification. When we show others that what we have to teach them can make their lives more varied and rewarding, they will be much more inclined to learn. In short, if we show persons ways they can feel effective to themselves, we have opened the door wider.

* * *

I have talked about these strategies of behavior and motivation in this order because they follow a set of assumptions I have made:

that we have a desire for autonomy and effectiveness in our "environment" and that many of us define our "environment" by the persons in it. Because we, as infants and children, had such a long period of dependency on others, we grow up with other persons as our known world. Often this period of dependence is extended for persons labelled retarded, and this makes the opinions and actions of others even more important.

Those who depend on others for support necessarily pay more attention to social strategy. A person who is successful in sales pays close attention to the reactions of the potential customer; politicians often take polls to learn what their constituencies are thinking. Dictators, absolute monarchs, and armed robbers pay far less attention to the feelings and needs of others.

Persons labelled retarded also can depend on others, but unlike articulate persons in sales or politicians with many opportunities to explain themselves, they often have less articulate expression and far less opportunity to use what they do have. As I have said, when words fail, actions often succeed. But rather than ask ourselves, "What is this person trying to get with this behavior?" we often label and dismiss the effort.

For example, rather than interpreting a situation as "Isn't it something how successful she is in making her needs known without language!" I have often heard, "She is so manipulative!" And what is it that these "manipulative" persons want? My own experience has been that they ask only for what I would consider minimal requests. Typically, these persons seem to be concerned about where they live, how they organize their time, and what they do for work. I have *never* encountered a person labelled retarded who had "manipulated" anyone out of large sums of money or had "manipulated" themselves into anything I would consider enviable.

Abnormal situations can misshape even the most ordinary wishes and ambitions. Most of the persons labelled retarded that I know live in circumstances that are not normal. To judge them in these extraordinary situations with ordinary criteria only emphasizes their differences. In working with others we are constantly teaching and learning. We need to teach others successful social strategies (through modeling, not through instruction), and we need to learn from others what they want to get with their social strategies. As it stands now, we often label behavior and forget the goal of it.

When someone says, "Oh, she only does that for attention," isn't that a little like saying, "You only talk to your friends because you're lonely"? When we talk to our friends, we may have many different motives, and we would resent giving all of them one label, especially a label that seems slightly desperate and condescending. Is it necessary to label a person's wish for contact—something I take as a given for everyone at some point—in such a negative way? I think it is more appreciative of others to see what they do as awkward perhaps, but an awkwardness that can diminish with training, the same way persons learning any new skill improve their performance with practice. When we have a more positive interpretation of another person's actions, we can encourage a more positive response.

How does a person settle on one strategy, like seeking attention, over another, like revenge? I think this question is frustrating if we think of persons in classes but rewarding if we think of persons individually. I am less interested in why persons who inappropriately demand attention do so than I am in learning why Kathy or Judy needs to. By asking about Kathy or Judy, we are looking at their lives and the sorts of situations and environments that might have made this strategy not merely successful but perhaps essential. Learning about another person's emotional realities is more important at this stage of our understanding than the development of a theoretical basis for it. Even if we had a perfect theoretical model for human behavior, we would still work with individuals and their specific challenges rather than with classes and their general problems.

These different possible motivations provide, for me, a plausible model for the ways that individuals act. I have assumed that most persons prefer either to be with others or to feel they can be when they want to. One of the worst punishments used in prisons is solitary confinement, which makes me think that most of us will go to great lengths to avoid social isolation. It seems that most persons like to be liked but if they cannot be liked they will accept being disliked, even despised, rather than being ignored. If some individuals confuse, irritate, frustrate, anger, or baffle us, then we may feel as defeated as those persons themselves do. The assumption is that they feel discouraged and isolated from others. But the strategies of luring us into a power struggle or showing us inadequacy or of demanding our attention all have one thing in common: they are ways of engaging us. If a person feels isolated from others, these ways are better than nothing to help lessen the sense of isolation.

In considering these various possibilities as motives, I think it is important to see how they all might be grounds for respecting rather than labelling others. A group of us were talking about a person who was presented as incapable of even the simplest task without a great deal of coaxing and encouragement. While she was quite capable of making lunch, she would need to be wheedled into doing so. As a way of developing an understanding of what this person seemed to need and how she seemed to see others, I mentioned the idea of displayed inadequacy as an effective (but sometimes annoying) social strategy. One of the persons in her residential program said, "You mean she's basically passive-agressive." Of course I did not. "Passive-aggressive" is a label, usually given to those we do not want to deal with. In that sense, it is not much different than calling someone a "bitch." The label gives us nothing except an excuse for avoiding persons by not taking their behavior seriously. Instead, I think of the strategies that irritate—attention, power, revenge, displaying inadequacy—as awkward and untrained rather than as ridiculous.

This consideration of motivation leaves several questions. For instance, is it important to differentiate between attention or power or revenge or the desire for effectance? I think not. These strategies themselves are different from one another, but the individuals who use them are even more so. I think it more important to use these ideas as a beginning in our attempt to understand others better. For instance, it is less useful to be able to say, "When Chad throws out his work, he is using revenge as a social strategy" than it is to be able to ask, "How do I feel when this happens? In what sort of position or with what way of looking at the world would I find acting like this helpful?" As I develop an understanding—or what I hope is an understanding—of this, I then ask, "How would I like to be approached if I found this strategy satisfying while those around me did not?" The only way to see if the answers to these questions are accurate is to check them out with the person himself. Using whatever we can, either language or behavior, we can see if our guesses are congruent with the person's own perceptions.

This discussion has considered ways we can better understand how and why *others* act the way they do by focusing on the social rather than the intrapsychic. To do this effectively, we need to understand ourselves and our roles. We can use our emotional reactions to others as giving clues as to how others are feeling. By doing so, we can temporarily avoid the problem of dealing with our "gut reactions" to a situation. For example, if Maria is frustrated by the effort it takes to get someone to listen to her and she resorts to throwing rocks, without knowing more details I have no idea if she is responding to a desire for attention, power, revenge, or effectiveness, or if she is expressing a general sense of inadequacy.

But with more information we can get a more detailed picture of how her life works for her. As a psychologist, the challenge I often feel is to develop an intervention that will respond primarily to her needs and not my own. So if she seems to be seeking constant attention, I might have fantasies of revenge but in reality try to help her get the attention in a more attractive way.

But in the long run I am concerned that all persons in the system have their needs considered. I think martyrdom and self-sacrifice are unnecessary for professional development. Indeed, I tend to think of those who suggest they are self-sacrificing as displaying a type of professional inadequacy. What are we supposed to do when we feel angry and discouraged with the persons we work for? Certainly, if we have such feelings and there is no hope of change for very long, we can expect to "burn out" and leave.

There are two avenues I can suggest, though there are undoubtedly more, that can help us better address our own feelings. One is to develop a relationship with others working either with you or in a setting similar to yours. Meet in your spare time in a relaxed environment away from work. If you can feel comfortable, then you can share your own sense of frustration as well as your triumphs and get credible validation for both. The networks of peer support I myself have are invaluable. Naturally, these persons are more to me than just "peer support." They are friends with whom I can safely share both my worst and best sides.

Another possibility, but I think this should be done carefully, is sharing feelings of frustration with the individuals we work for. I say "carefully" only because I am eager to avoid blaming the "victim." By this I mean that my inability to understand a person is something we both share, and I would have no interest in suggesting it is the other person's "fault." But there are times when I will say, "I don't understand what is going on with you right now" and then ask the person to give me more information to use. I have found it helpful to admit to a person, "Your way of dealing with this leaves me in the dark. How can we help?" ("This" can be anything from being assaultive to being indifferent.)

We are all in a dialogue with the world we know. If we see that world as being generous and considerate, we probably respond more kindly than if we see the world as deceitful and mean-spirited. Of course, others react to us in the same way. If we are seen as friendly, we are often treated as friends, which in turn encourages our good-natured ways. I suppose this process begins right at birth so that a "good" baby who never cries and is lavished with affection grows up seeing the world as a more pleasant place than does a "colicky" baby whose demands are met with resentment. If we think of this process for persons with special needs, it is easy to see how misunderstandings can arise from the start. If some children need more or have difficulty in expressing themselves, then others might treat them as if they were "babyish" or "unsociable" or any other misinterpretation that can be placed on those who cannot explain themselves fully and accurately.

One assumption I have made is that most persons try to be effective in their environments and, for most of us, that environment is largely shaped by the other persons in it. Because of the long period of dependence that babies have on others, I think we learn very early in life that others are a given, if not a necessity. So I tend to assume most of us need not only to be effective in general, but to be effective with other persons in particular. This is why I see "motives" as strategies to that goal.

If we think of individuals with special needs as most often seeing and hearing more than they can say, then it is easy to see how these strategies for social involvement can become maladaptive. If our culture pays lavish attention to those who have good expressive skills, musicians, film makers, novelists, for example; if it rewards some with powers to make decisions; if it admires competence in physical or intellectual challenge; then the persons labelled retarded have typically been shut out of ordinary avenues of social exchange.

Major Points Relating to Competence

The desire to have an effect on one's environment is a strong and common motivation. As such, it can be used as a reinforcer in helping others acquire and develop skills.

The desire for competence is another basis for respecting others. If we want to feel growth and accomplishment from our jobs, then we can understand others wanting this as well. This provides a challenge to professionals to satisfy more than just "training needs."

Skill grows from skill. Helping a person to develop a sense of effectiveness can encourage generalizing that sense of competence to other areas as well. A person who is good in working with things can use that as the basis for learning to work well with others.

Being effective in something is rewarding to individuals on their own terms. Rather than praise such persons for doing well, it is more effective to congratulate them on the sense of accomplishment their success can give them.

—5—

Medical Issues

Paul could not speak and had virtually no other way to communicate. He could not stand or sit up on his own; so he was kept in a wheelchair. When Paul began moaning constantly, this was interpreted as "demanding attention." The persons working with him decided to ignore this "inappropriate behavior." In spite of this, Paul began screaming. He presented such a "management problem" that he was moved from his usual position near the nurses' station to a more remote part of the ward so as not to disturb others. He was described as "manipulative" and "spoiled." Later, during a routine X ray, he was found to have such advanced degeneration of his spinal disks that he was presumed to be in intense pain.

The section on motivation emphasized understanding how a person's challenges might be functionally adaptive. Approaches were considered to help us use a person's behavior as communication. This can establish a dialogue to help a person feel more effective. To do this, though, we must first understand what a person is trying to get. Paul would not have felt significantly better if we had in fact paid all the attention we could to him. His screams were a response to pain. Our best assistance would have been to alleviate that pain.

This section will discuss ways in which a person can be responding to physical demands. Whenever a person uses a consistent "behavior" regardless of what the external environment is, one can reasonably guess that this person is responding either to a physical or an internal stimulus.

109

Sometimes a person is described as doing something for "no reason." This is hard to believe. I assume all behavior responds in some way either to the outer world we all share or to a person's inner world. When a person is described as doing something for "no reason," I assume this means, "I can't think of any reason for doing that." Obviously, these are two very different points of reference. Paul's "screaming behavior" must have been a puzzle to those who worked with him. One wonders what those who labelled him "manipulative" were thinking when they did that. Was it frustration at being incapable of helping him or arrogance that they could know with complete certainty the reasons for his actions? Was it laziness for not trying to find some cause, or was it the simple and cold ignorance that dismisses another person's cries for help?

An extreme example like Paul's points up two important considerations when we are presented with behavioral challenges: Is it possible that this behavior is in response to an undetected physical discomfort or to a physically related disorder? Is there an alternative interpretation for what we are observing that would lead to an alternative treatment?

These questions are important because, if a person indeed does have a physical disorder, it should be treated. Obviously, this will not happen if we interpret a person's physical illness as "attention seeking." Sometimes we speculate about knowing what is going on and act on that guess. Trial and error is a practical necessity. But sometimes we act as if we really do know what is going on and act on our "convictions." This courts unnecessary suffering.

When persons cannot explain their situation on their own, it is important for us to consider many different functions that a "challenging behavior" could be serving. A "team approach" often develops a consensus, and only one guess is made. Some professionals and groups of professionals seem to do the same thing for everyone: everyone needs a "behavior plan" or "medication" or "intensive one-to-one therapy." All of these are useful tools to have available, but none of them works for everyone always. One danger to our professional competence is to become automatically responsive rather than truly considerate. When we look for ways to use a favorite intervention rather than ways to help the situation—in all its complexity—then we are running the risk not only of failing to find the solution but of worsening the problem.

One way to help foster this process is to make clear and keep clear that if persons are not telling us what their behavior means, then we can never really know for certain. Given this uncertainty, there are no "right answers"; there are only guesses more likely to help improve the situation. Training and experience can help us see some patterns of adaptation as typical. But those of us who work directly with the persons being considered often have specific and useful information. Sometimes these views coincide, but sometimes they do not. Rather than politicize this process, though, by trying to make our work a way of showing who is right and who is wrong, it is easier to work on finding a respectful and helpful approach. If one approach is more effective than another, the triumph is not that one person is smarter or more professional, but rather that we have helped the person we set out to help.

Sometimes looking for physical illness is the obvious place to begin. If a person has a problem with bed wetting, then we are first concerned that it is not due to some physical dysfunction. But when it seems that the bedwetting is not based on a physical cause, we move with more confidence to thinking of it as an issue that we can help the person with through training. But we should not move with *too much* confidence. Just because we cannot find a physical basis for a behavior does not mean it is not there.* This is especially true of persons who do not have good verbal skills. Sometimes the persons we work with, much like the rest of us, forget what all the symptoms that disturbed them were when they visit a physician, or they will under- or overestimate the seriousness or frequency of them.

Distinguishing between mind and body, between mental health and physical health, can be a disservice to persons labelled retarded because their difficulties are often treated as purely mental (that is, their behavior is motivated by "attention seeking") or purely physical (their behavior is treated chemically). This distorts the reality of actual life. Have you ever had an experience that was purely mental or purely physical? Angels, I suppose, can be "pure mind'; only corpses "pure body." Even something that seems as straightforwardly physical as a common cold sometimes seems to be connected with stress. And if stress can make us, perhaps, more susceptible to disease, it certainly seems reasonable that chronic disease can itself be stressful.

---

*It is sometimes forgotten that one cannot prove a negative. You cannot prove, for example, that there is no Santa Claus. Similarly, no physician can say something absolutely is *not* physical. All we can ever say with any confidence is that no physical cause for a behavior has been found.

Persons labelled retarded have the same give-and-take with the environment the rest of us do. If we feel depressed, we usually can locate either a primarily physical or a psychological cause. An active person who is confined to bed for some months will feel depressed because of this physical cause, just as the person who has lost a valued relationship will feel depressed by the primarily psychological cause. Persons who can express themselves can discuss these factors in therapy. For persons with expressive challenges, the interplay between physical and psychological factors often gets ignored, and only one side of this relation is considered. As a result, such persons often get service that is irrelevant to their situations. Paul needed medical assistance but was given a psychological interpretation instead. Similarly, those persons who behave in confusing—but more especially frightening—ways often get chemotherapy instead of some psychological consideration. Giving persons medication for behavior presumes that there is nothing disturbing in the environment (which we, for the most part, are responsible for) but rather that the persons treated are themselves disturbed. This can be tantamount to blaming a victimized person for complaining aloud.

The label of retardation is technically based on intellectual and social functioning.* By definition, this "diagnosis" is not made by a physician but by a psychologist. On the other hand, the vast majority of persons labelled retarded have a physical disorder that has caused their developmental delays. Since physicians diagnose physical disorders, they can then predict that a given child will be labelled retarded, though they cannot predict at all to what degree a person's skills will be affected by this. For example, most persons with Down's Syndrome are identified at birth. But to know that certain babies have Down's Syndrome tells us relatively little about what their lives will be like since there is a large range of abilities among persons with this diagnosis.

Regardless of what the causes of retardation might be, they are medically irreversible; so there has been little for medicine to do about them per se. If a person labelled retarded has a routine med-

---

*Mental retardation is currently based on three criteria: "(1) significantly subaverage general intellectual functioning, (2) resulting in, or associated with, deficits or impairments in adaptive behavior, (3) with onset before the age of 18. The diagnosis is made regardless of whether or not there is a coexisting mental or physical disorder." (American Psychiatric Association 1980)

ical problem, a broken leg, for example, then the treatment indicated is also routine.

But if persons labelled retarded are upset or depressed or feel emotions that are troubling, their treatment might be very different from the treatment a person without handicaps might receive. Many variables combine to make critical differences in therapy. These include how articulate the person is, how easily the person can establish a relationship with a therapist, and how much the person can pay. It seems only common sense to point out that wealthy, attractive, articulate persons often get better treatment not only from the health community but from life in general than do persons with little or no money, who look "different," have difficulty in explaining themselves, or seem difficult to establish rapport with. In this sense, the medical community reflects the community at large in its approach to persons labelled retarded.

This book assumes that we cannot help others in a meaningful and sustained way without forming a working relationship with them. Most of us find it easier to form positive relationships with those persons we readily understand than with persons we have a difficult time talking to. Most health care providers are not different in this. Furthermore, health care is more often provided with an eye to efficiency than it is through established relationships. This system might provide better health services for most persons, but for those labelled retarded, this can be a source of misunderstanding. Psychiatrists, for example, sometimes do not even see the person they treat, much less get to understand *what* they are treating. This is often true in institutional settings, where the psychiatrist relies on the nurse who relies on those working in direct service. This sort of grapevine can distort and omit critical information, which can lead to inappropriate treatment.

An interview, of course, is no guarantee of proper treatment.*

---

*When I first started my training, I would sometimes attend staff meetings at a state hospital. The psychiatrist would interview patients for medication review or discharge in front of a dozen or so persons. Occasionally, though, the list of persons to be seen was short, and he would routinely "interview" a person who had been hospitalized for many years and for whom there were no real plans for discharge. In one instance he asked a man with schizophrenia if he had any concerns. The man did: Would he get to the county fair and could he go home for Christmas? This was in the middle of the summer. The fair was held in October. Afterward, the psychiatrist remarked on this man's poor contact with reality. But a nurse, fortunately, pointed out that this man was interviewed once a year at the most. His asking was actually good planning.

Many persons find it difficult to express their feelings. Pamela had been receiving large doses of an antipsychotic medication for many years. She started getting this when she lived in an institution, and the prescription followed her to her group home and her new, local psychiatrist. Every two months, he would "interview" her and ask, "How are you doing?" She took this to be a simple social inquiry, but the psychiatrist took it to be her assessment of her actual state of mind. She invariably answered "Okay."

Her psychiatrist never asked her specifics such as, "How are you getting along at work? Do you find it easy to concentrate? How much are you sleeping each day? Are you sleeping more than usual? How's your appetite? Do you ever feel grouchy with others? When and with whom? Why do you think that is? In other words, the psychiatrist did not look for signs of over- or undermedication, of current psychological challenges, and so on. Instead, he would note in her chart, "Pamela remains stabilized on her present medication" and then give her a prescription for another 60-day supply. If Pamela lost her temper (that is, if she were to shout at someone) the persons working in her group home would call up and get an order from her psychiatrist for an increase in her dosage. The psychiatrist would do this without seeing Pamela until her next visit with him.

All the persons in this system were working as they thought they should. Pamela thought she should take her meds as prescribed; the persons working in her home thought they should be responsible for seeing that Pamela's medications were available to her and to report changes in behavior; and the psychiatrist felt that, having established a treatment where Pamela could function comfortably, he should monitor it regularly to see that this equilibrium was maintained.

In the course of a year, there was a complete turnover of those

---

One more anecdote should be mentioned. A man had been charged with a crime and sent to a state psychiatric facility for observation. After several days he was told that the psychiatrist would interview him, specifically to determine his defense at the trial. He spoke without interruption for an hour, describing in detail how his relationship with his wife Debbie, his abuse of alcohol, and his long stretch of unemployment had contributed to the emotional stresses and his confused state of mind at the time of his alleged crime. The interviewing psychiatrist listened. Finally, at the end of the hour, he asked, "Vot is a *Debbie*?"

working in Pamela's group home. These new workers had an entirely different view of chemotherapy. They had felt their job was to get everyone they worked with off medications as rapidly as possible. They saw themselves as "protecting the retarded against medication." As a result, they told the psychiatrist to discontinue Pamela's prescription. He thought they should maintain the success they had. Rather than negotiating this with him, though, some of them started to "forget" Pamela's medication occasionally. Sometimes, Pamela would go several days in a row without getting her medication. She started to experience unpredictable mood swings. Since some of the direct service providers did not know about this new "schedule" for Pamela's medication, they reported their concern to the psychiatrist who in turn *increased* her prescribed dosage. Pamela's behavior became sufficiently erratic that the group home supervisors—who were unaware of what was happening—asked that she be admitted to the local psychiatric unit.

The use of medication sometimes becomes an emotional issue. But medication is neither "good" nor "bad" any more than behaviorism or surgery or a walk around the block is "good" or "bad." The value of these interventions depends on how they are used. But the use of medication, like most emotionally charged issues, seems to provoke absolute and extreme positions. Some feel that all medications are punishing and should never be given; others imagine medication to be the best way to approach any behavior we wish would go away. What is needed is not a debate on medications, pro and con. Since there are those who demonstrably profit from chemotherapy, it would seem wasteful to say that no one should ever be given medication. On the other hand, it seems equally naive to think that all behavioral challenges are best treated medically. The question is not, "Are meds good or bad?" but rather, "How can we best use them?"

The system we use in working with challenging behaviors itself seems challenging. By definition, "challenging behaviors" tax whatever skills we have. And when we are at a loss as to which step is best next to take, there is more room for guesswork than for certainty. The result of this predicament is that we are often forced into action without knowing quite what we are doing. There are some typical situations in which persons are commonly treated with medication. Seizure disorders, for example, generally (though not always) benefit most from chemotherapy. Some types of seizure disorder can cause aggressive behaviors. These aggressions are not the result of situational turmoil but the result of a neurological condition. Sometimes persons experience depressions so severely that they are unable to respond effectively to their environments. Antidepressant medication can help such persons regain their energies and skills to make the changes necessary in their lives. Sometimes persons experience hallucinations or bursts of uncontrollable energy. These situations are thought to be physical responses that are best treated chemically.

For example, if Frank starts to hit otherss or to hurt himself and there is no reason that he can explain to us or that we can find for this behavior, we will all have different immediate responses. Some persons will ignore him or time him out, hoping not to reinforce this situation with undue attention; others will want to try spending more time with Frank in order to increase their understanding of what he might be experiencing; some will want to get orders for a p.r.n. medication.*

What is needed in this instance is a meeting with Frank and as many of those who know him and have some familiarity with the sorts of challenges he might be having. This is important because the first stages of our thinking often determine the options we finally consider seriously. If we are missing important information about Frank, then we will start to make decisions based on faulty or inadequate observations. For example, it might be that Frank is really upset about something that happens during the workday. If we think only of what has happened at home, then we will have overlooked the biggest contributing factor to Frank's difficulties.

But suppose that everyone who works with Frank agrees that they can find no apparent causes for his being upset. For the sake of this hypothetical example, we can also rely on physical and neurological assessment to rule out these areas as apparently "causing" his "behavior." So, for lack of a better solution, we begin to consider medication as a way of helping Frank maintain better control.

The first consideration, I think, is *what* do we want to medicate *for*? This asks us to be specific. If we really wish to give someone a drug to make that person less "obnoxious," we are best advised to obtain moderate quantities of something strong and drink it ourselves.

If asking *what* we want to medicate is the question, then

P.r.n. (*pro re nata*): as needed or, literally, as things arise.

it seems important that anyone who has information about the person to be treated (especially the person to be treated) should be present during the diagnostic process. I emphasize this because diagnosis determines treatment.

It sometimes happens that a person is referred for medication because he is "moody." This is obviously too vague a problem. Is Frank moody because he is depressed? And if he is depressed, has something happened to challenge his coping skills (like major changes in his life)? Or did this depression "just happen"? Does he need medication to help him through this depression, or would he be better served with help in learning assertiveness or communications skills? It does not make sense to "treat" chemically anyone who has a depression without asking, or trying to find out, if there are reasons for the depression. And if we can find the reasons, does it make sense for such a person to take a medication for something *we* can help change? Or is Frank excited, restless, talkative, and unable to sleep for more than a few hours for weeks at a time and then he has periods of lethargy where he is indifferent to things that formerly pleased him? In this case, he might have episodes of manic-depression. Or is he seen as moody because some days he is friendly when he comes home from work and other days he prefers to sit in his room watching soap operas? In that case he might just be "being Frank" and need no "treatment" at all.

Whenever we feel we have run out of social, emotional, or intellectual reasons for a person's behavior, we might understandably try to find physical explanations. Before referring Frank to a medical provider because "something is wrong" with him, it would be useful for the persons concerned, preferably as a group, to identify what exactly causes their concern. It will be more useful to be able to say, "Frank slept no more than two hours a night last week, did not eat breakfast or lunch, and spoke about unrealistic plans; that is, he was leaving for Spain to marry the Queen...." This sort of attention to frequency and specifics helps more than a referral that reads, "Frank has been feeling grandiose and agitated recently." Frank could have felt "grandiose and agitated" if someone had insulted him at dinner and he left the table in tears shouting, "Leave me alone! I don't have to take this!" The specifics of one situation suggest a disorder (mania) that can be effectively treated with lithium carbonate, while the other points toward a social unpleasantness that can be addressed by Frank and the persons he lives with.

It is even more useful if these behaviors can be put into a context. For instance, the statement "Frank struck Max for no reason" is much less informative than "Frank and Max were watching TV when he walked over and pinched his arm. When he was asked why he did this, he only shrugged."

Typically, when we are challenged in our work, we bring in an outside source of information for a consultation. If we need a working relationship with the persons we are serving, we also need an understanding with the persons who help in this role. Sometimes consultants are expected to "fix" Frank's "problem." Or else, they are expected to endorse a solution already worked out. If a group of persons working with Frank tells a consultant to come up with "a behavior plan" or to prescribe meds for Frank's "acting out," they have made themselves and their recommendation—as well as Frank's challenges—an issue. The consultant is better used as a moderator of different perspectives. From a combination of these points of view, the consultant can help to develop a plan that is respectful of Frank's needs as well as those of the persons working with him. In other words, the consultant can be part of a process of helping rather than of fixing."

Some persons who work in direct service are meticulous in gathering specifics for consideration. Before they can present their information, though, they explain, "We've been challenged lately by Frank. He's hit others and we are worried because...."

"Frank is agitated and assaultive? Let's try Mellaril 50 mg. three times a day." And before the specifics of the situation are presented, Frank has a new "treatment plan."

Sometimes persons who work in direct service feel less important than the persons they are consulting. As a result, they are reluctant to ask questions because they feel they are taking up too much time. This leads to a lack of information, which can lead to unpleasant conclusions.* If a consultant of any sort hurries over an explanation before putting a recommendation into effect, then either another consultation—or another consultant—is needed.

Medication rarely does just what is intended and nothing more. If a person we are working with is recommended for chemotherapy, then what are the side effects we should expect? The major antipsychotics, for instance, have side effects (often called tardive dyskinesia or Parkinsonian side effects) that cannot yet be

---

*The great tragedies of literature are, among other things, about poor information flow. Oedipus learns too late the critical fact; Hamlet too early.

predicted by age, gender, diagnosis, or amount of medication prescribed. Unfortunately, once these side effects appear, they are permanent. They can be controlled symptomatically, but once the person stops taking the medication for the side effects, then the symptoms return. Other side effects are less dramatic but no less important. For example, a person might experience a dry mouth or constipation as side effects. Both of these are relatively simple to manage, but they need to be known about before they can be addressed.

Even if a provider lists some of the more common side effects of a medication, an individual might have a relatively rare response. To see if this is likely to be due to the chemotherapy or to something else, there are two valuable books to have ready access to: the *Physician's Desk Reference* (the *PDR*) and a medical dictionary.

The *PDR* catalogues drugs in current use. The entries include a description of the drug, when it should be used (e.g., "for the treatment of multiple vitamin deficiencies"), when it should not be used (e.g., "contraindicated for persons with renal, hepatic or bone-marrow damage"), warnings about it (e.g., "may be habit forming"), precautions to be taken (e.g., "should not follow X-ray therapy or other radiomimetic drugs"), descriptions of adverse reactions and side effects (e.g., "torticollis, nausea, or diarrhea"), usual dosages (e.g., "30 mg. b.i.d."), description of the effects of an overdose (e.g., "loss of consciousness, lowered blood pressure"), and the forms it usually is supplied in (e.g., "bottles of 50 black and yellow capsules").

Many of the terms used in the *PDR* are technical; so a medical dictionary for unfamiliar language is helpful. But if any person, either just beginning or in an advanced stage of chemotherapy, were to complain of nausea, getting medical attention is a commonsense procedure. But even experienced providers sometimes overlook physical distress as a side effect to medication.

Taking note of the potential side effects is useful when a new medication is begun. But it is important also to establish *when* or *how* the effect of the medication is to be assessed. Many times, a person is given chemotherapy, and if the original "problem" disappears, then the person is kept on it, sometimes for *decades*. One woman I worked with had been given the same drugs for 30 years without change. All medications have some element of risk; so it is important to establish what the chemotherapy is intended to do.

A medication should first be assessed for effectiveness as soon as it should be taking effect. If, by our previously defined definition of success, it is working, then we should see that as giving the person a chance to learn a new way of dealing with life's challenges. What often happens, though, is once a medication is thought to be "working" the person stays on it for years. This can be defended only as providing a convenience for the persons working with him and not as a sensible approach for the person medicated. No medication should be used to "manage behavior" for life. So one ought to establish some time limit as to how long it will be given.

Let us consider a purely hypothetical example. We have tried every change of the environment and social system we can think of to help Frank with his behavioral challenges. In spite of our best intervention, he continues for no *apparent* reason to shout loudly and throw things and hit others. His neurological workup states his neurological functioning is within normal limits.*

When persons concerned about Frank consult with a physician, he recommends Drugitol, but when we ask about side effects and contraindications, he says that the only contraindications are for persons with liver damage. Frank had hepatitis three years ago; so the physician changes the prescription to Neodrugitol. He cautions that this medication interacts with milk to cause nausea. So a note is made to make certain that Frank gets juice instead of milk. We then establish how we will know whether this drug is helpful. The baseline data show that Frank had five episodes of shouting, three of throwing things, and two of hitting others in the last ten days. We would expect "improvement" if the drug is effective. Neodrugitol takes five days to reach therapeutic level. "Improvement" in this case could be defined as a 50 percent reduction from baseline of these episodes.

There is obviously no set standard for what constitutes improvement, but the health provider and the persons monitoring the behavior should have some sense of what can realistically be expected as a change if the medication is working. If Frank is taking the maximum safe dosage of Neodrugitol and getting only a slight change in his behavior, then his medication should be reconsi-

---

*Again, it is important to keep in mind that even with this report he may yet have a neurological disorder that leads to this behavior. The science of neurology is still in its relatively imprecise and formative stages.

dered. The negotiation as to what is a satisfactory improvement should be between the severity of the behavior and the severity of the side effects. Large doses of a psychotropic (such as chlorpromazine, also known as Thorazine) can produce irreversible neurological damage. For example, persons, who have many episodes of harming themselves or others and are chronically kept on locked wards can live independently provided they take their medication. This sort of life might well be less than ideal, but the benefits for such persons would seem to outweigh the possible losses. But these individuals are taking large doses of psychotropics because they are easier to "manage" by the person working on the locked wards, then we have to ask if the risks to these individuals really outweigh the benefits to the providers.

Another important part of establishing in advance what would constitute "improvement" is a time limit for it to take place. Many drugs take effect within minutes or hours, others within days or weeks. But it is important to know when it should have taken effect if it is going to. Otherwise, a drug might be discontinued before it has had a chance to be effective (as is sometimes the case with the antidepressants), or it might be given indefinitely with the vague hopes that someday it will help.

In Frank's case, if his behavior "improves" (here defined as a 50 percent reduction in the frequency of target behaviors) then another time limit should be used: how long will Frank have to learn new social strategies with medication before he can be expected to use them without it? Once a person is no longer "a problem," there is an understandable tendency not to change. But if we remember that no drug is without side effects, then we must constantly justify giving it. As it is now, the prevailing tendency is to ask for justification for *discontinuing* the drug.

If Frank can reduce by 50 percent the frequency* of target behaviors and maintain this success for three months, then he could be gradually removed from the drug and see what, if any, changes

---

*Frequency is just one consideration. I have used it here because, once a behavior is defined, it is easier to get agreement on the number of times it occurs. In this example, though, another realistic consideration would be "intensity," but that would be a subjective assessment and far less simple to establish.

this makes in his ability to function appropriately. If the frequency were to return to baseline levels, then he could be reintroduced to the drug and reassessed with the same "drug holiday" procedure as before. A year is a practical limit on the time a person can go without a "drug holiday." This could be true of seizure medications as well.

On the other hand, Frank may take the Neodrugitol faithfully and have no change in his behavior. This, of course, is a simpler decision to make: it should be discontinued and another type of therapy tried, using the same procedures of review.

One word of caution must be added. Medications for "behavior" are the least defensible use of them. Persons with seizure disorders have a diagnosable condition that can be helped with chemotherapy. But a person who "acts out" does not have this. Often when we resort to the use of medications for what are essentially social situations, we are reinforcing for ourselves and the medical community the idea that persons labelled retarded cannot learn new social skills; so they need to be "managed" chemically. Can we really claim that we have tried *everything* to help a person? What we might mean is that we have done all we can do, but there are other environments and other persons to work with. Sometimes a person's behavioral challenges are a direct result of an environment—Frank does not like the persons he lives with, or he is sensitive to loud noise and he lives with noisy persons, for example. Realistically, what often happens is that Frank will get medication rather than a new place to live because the medication is by far the easier solution to arrange. We must always be prepared to explain that the use of medication, indeed the use of any approach we try, is not merely the most *convenient* but the most *helpful.*

Suppose that Frank has just moved into a home, and he arrives with a large bottle of pills with instructions to give them to him four times a day. There is no specific reason given for his taking them or, if there is, he has been taking them without a break for the last five years. What next?

One reasonable suggestion would be a "drug holiday." One immediate precaution, though, would be to ask of this would be fair, given the sudden major change in his life. So it might be prudent to wait until Frank gets a chance to establish a routine in his new life. Also, if the persons he now lives with are relatively new to him, it would be wise to give him a chance to get to know them better. But as soon as Frank feels comfortable with his new life, then he should be consulted as to how he feels about discontinuing chemotherapy.*

Frank, of course, should be consulted. Some persons *appear* to have no understanding of the life around them, but my experience is that this appearance is often deceiving and we more often underestimate than overestimate a person's skills. Frank may, in fact, have no opinion about taking medication, but it is important for him to tell us that rather than assuming it ourselves. Some persons are quite capable of understanding the reasons for a drug holiday and can be eager to try it. Others interpret this as punishment since they will not be getting their pills anymore. By talking these things over in advance, we can help this transition either with information or a different routine. If persons are feeling deprived because they are not getting their pills in the morning, then they can be consulted as to what they would like to have instead. There are many possible responses, of course, to this situation. We should avoid making guesses and assumptions, and let the persons involved make the response that they need.

Once we have negotiated the drug holiday with the person taking the medication, we should consult with a medical provider, preferably the person who has been renewing the prescription, as to how the drug holiday can be managed. Some persons will be able to discontinue their medication immediately; others will have to be weaned gradually.

Suppose, though, the provider refuses to discuss discontinuing the medication. This is when a second opinion is helpful.

* * *

---

*Before consulting Frank, though, we should make certain which drugs we are asking him to take a holiday from. Certain drugs are necessary for the maintenence of health: antihypertensives (blood pressure medication), for example. Few persons would seriously argue that a life-sustaining medication should be discontinued to see if it really is sustaining life. The issue more often concerns drugs for "behavior." Since persons can grow and learn new behaviors over time, the short-term use of these drugs can give a person sufficient control to learn new skills. But after a certain period of time (a maximum of one year), one needs verification that the person still needs medication to maintain comfortable self-control.

Hugh was a hunched over, clinically obese man described as "socially withdrawn." When he would meet someone new, he would hunch over even more and refuse to make eye contact or to speak. If he was asked a question directly, he would shrug. He had been described as "lazy" and "manipulative" because he seemed never to have any energy except when he wanted something. When Hugh lived in a state training school, he would occasionally express his anger by throwing things. Apparently, no one asked him the reasons he was irritated or angry. This behavior was labelled "tantrumming," and the persons working most directly with him recommended that he receive medication. Over 20 years later, Hugh had moved to a community residence and was still taking the same medication and the same dosage: Mellaril three times a day "for behavior." He was also taking Artane for the Parkinsonian side effects of this chemotherapy. The Parkinsonian side effects were his moving his fingers in "pill rolling."

The supervisor of his community apartment became indignant. She felt that medications of all sorts were improperly used and badly reviewed. Accordingly, she told Hugh's psychiatrist that Hugh should be stopped immediately from any further medication. His psychiatrist agreed and within a few days Hugh was shouting, throwing dishes, and generally frightening others. He was immediately put back on medication, and the persons working with him decided that he really did need to be maintained on Mellaril.

In the course of a year, all of the persons working in the home had been replaced. The new persons also wondered if the medications Hugh was getting were necessary. Betty, the new supervisor, asked Hugh's psychiatrist if he could have a change or a reduction in medication. He agreed to reduce the dosage from three times a day to once at bedtime. In the course of a few months, they noticed that this man, who had been seen so negatively, was actually capable of being companionable. Hugh became more energetic and more involved in his apartment's activities.

One of his friends at work suggested they join a gym so that together they could get some help in diet and exercise. For the first few visits, someone went with Hugh to help him get information on the program, but after these initial visits Hugh took a cab over on his own. This was the most independent project he had ever undertaken, and he took obvious pride in telling others how much he felt he had accomplished in making this step alone. The recommendations of those working at the gym were also successful for Hugh in their stated goals: he started losing the two or three pounds a week he had wanted to lose. After several months, he looked (and said he felt) like a different person.

In spite of these positive changes, he still had moments of being irritable and irritating. While some of the persons who worked with him were pleased by his progress, others began to think of him as being "spoiled." They wondered if this were not his "real" personality and if reducing the medication had just allowed him more energy to be "difficult." These persons wanted to know if they could expect Hugh to change his "difficult" behavior.

One useful assumption to make is that no one wants to be obnoxious or, more accurately, socially ineffective. When any of us is challenging to be with, though, it is more useful to assume that we do not know or trust another social strategy to be reliable in dealing with others.

It was at this juncture that I started working with Hugh in therapy. He presented himself as someone interested in learning about himself and how he could change; so we started on a positive note. After a few initial visits where we were learning to know one another better, he explained to me how concerned he was about his family. His father was terminally ill with a degenerative heart disease. His brother had had a minor role in an illegal operation, and he was worried about how this would be resolved. His family seemed quite close (they talked daily on the phone), and these events made him feel helpless and anxious. He had been reluctant to share the depth of concerns with others partly because he was embarrassed by his brother's difficulties and partly because he was afraid of losing emotional control in talking about them.

Rather than talking with those he shared daily life with, he showed his anxiety in being short-tempered with sudden changes of mood. My understanding of his situation was that this would be the predictable reaction for many persons under such stress. But Hugh had never faced emotional stresses without medication. Now that he had less medication, I saw him as having the energy to respond to his emotional life more directly for the first time since adolescence. Not surprisingly, then, he was using fairly unskilled ways of expressing himself and his concerns.

This still left the problem of how Hugh was going to be able to live more comfortably with others. With Hugh's permission, I explained (without going into detail) to those concerned for him that he was under a great deal of emotional stress. They had heard a little of his brother's difficulty, and they already knew more about his father's condition. Thus they could easily understand his feeling stressed.

One approach I thought might be useful would be for these persons to share with him their own experiences of how they felt worried about losses and other stresses in their lives and how they responded, both badly and well. This would show how concerned they really were for him and at the same time show him that we all have stresses and that we all handle some better than others.

As for the medication review, we wondered if his medication at bedtime was not essentially a sedative for him to get a good night's rest. Instead of this dosage, we worked with his psychiatrist for yet another plan. As a result of this consultation, it was decided to try giving him a 10 milligram tablet in the morning and leaving it up to him whether he needed it or not. At first, there was concern that he would just take it because it had been given to him. But if this happened, we would then recommend that he try a day without it and see if he felt any different. Some worried that he would not know how to manage this responsibility on his own. I encouraged them to anticipate that—at first—he probably could not or would not comfortably deal with this new responsibility. But without the opportunity for self-management, we could easily guarantee that he would never learn what the medication could and could not do for him. Only Hugh could learn the effect of the drug and—like the rest of us—he would have to learn by trial and error. How did any of us learn to take aspirin—or whatever drugs we use? We try them and rely on the effect to judge whether we should try them again. Some persons, for example, insist that a certain brand of common medication will work much better than another brand of essentially the same drug. If we have choices of which medication is most effective for us, it is because we have tried the drugs ourselves. Persons labelled retarded are rarely given choices of medication and are generally not consulted as to which they find most effective for them.

The worst that could happen in this case would be that Hugh would routinely take the medication prescribed anyway. But the point of offering him a choice was to give him a message with the drug. By asking him if he needed to take it on a given day, we were asking a genuine question—one that only he could answer. My experience in working with Hugh was that he had difficulty in identifying how he really felt about a situation. He had been, as is often the case for persons labelled retarded, oversocialized. He had been trained to say what he thought he *should* feel rather than what he actually *did* feel. If we had removed the message "Good people take their medication when told" and replaced it with "Responsible people take medication when they need to," we would be reinforcing the idea that he was the best judge of his own needs and feelings. My hope was that by beginning with something concrete—how he felt physically—this awareness would then begin to generalize to less tangible areas such as how he felt emotionally.

Sometimes a drug holiday will provoke some unpleasant behaviors. But there are (currently) no prescription drugs for "unpleasantness." If a person has had no opportunity to learn how to be irritated appropriately or how to handle ordinary stress in socially acceptable ways, then returning him to medication is not the answer. Instead, we need to have patience and skill in showing that irritation and stress are not remarkable and that we all can learn to deal with these more or less successfully. If a person has been on a psychotropic medication (Mellaril, Thorazine, Stelazine, and so on) for six years, that means for the last six years that person has not been exposed to stress without the intervention of the drug. Once the medication is removed, this unfamiliar stress may seem—at first—overwhelming and unmanageable.

There comes a time when we can negotiate with the person if or when the medication should be resumed. But this would be done in the same way as beginning chemotherapy; that is, a specific set of target behaviors would be established and monitored to see if the drug is doing what it is supposed to do. The hazard with this system is that it can make managing a person with drugs more convenient for those making the decision. It is small wonder, then, that so many of the persons we work with get medication.

> Alex had lived for almost ten years in a psychiatric hospital where he had been labelled a hebephrenic schizophrenic. He would spend his days pacing the hallways or walking around in circles, his head tilted as if listening to something, laughing or frowning as he muttered words that no one else could hear. Sometimes, he would lash out with his left hand, striking anything or anyone in the way. This made him appear not only strange but dangerous. As a result, no one spent any length of time with him. His social contacts were restricted to getting his medication from the nurse and being "escorted" to a seclusion room for hitting others.

In serving persons who have been labelled either "retarded" or "psychotic," neurology and neuropsychology are often overlooked. Since the physical basis for a person's retardation always, at some point, involves the central nervous system, then it makes sense to understand a person's neurological status as much as we can. The reason this is important is not because adding new labels improves treatment. It is important because some of the labels that neurologists use are treatable—unlike the label "retarded," which is a status and not a disease, or the label "psychotic," which might be a disease but for which we have no cure.

When the nurses explained the challenges Alex was presenting, they asked me to develop a "behavioral plan" for him. Those who worked with Alex assumed that he was responding to hallucinations. Their initial response to this hypothesis was to get an increase in his antipsychotic medication (Thorazine), but now he was getting such large dosages that to give him more seemed to be more likely to present a health hazard than to decrease his hallucinations. Since they assumed that his hallucinations could be the only cause for his actions, they wanted to use behavior modification as a way of controlling him.

Often, perhaps from habit, we take our assumptions as fact. The assumption here was that Alex was responding to hallucinations as part of his "psychosis." Therefore, he should be given antipsychotic drugs. But if this assumption were true, would it not seem likely that he would respond favorably to those drugs? Instead of asking why we are medicating when the medication has no effect, we stay with our initial hypothesis rather than discontinue the medication. This is why I emphasize the importance of defining target behaviors as a way of seeing if medication is successful. If we are medicating for hallucinations and these do not decrease, we need either a new medication or none.

This was one reason I was reluctant to try to modify Alex's behavior. I did not know why he was doing it or, more precisely, what his behavior meant to him. If Alex were using these strategies for social goals, I thought this would be clear to those who knew him well. On the other hand, if he were acting this way for "no reason," then these behaviors might be his response to a neurological condition over which he had no control.

I asked those who worked with Alex if he had or seemed to have any stomach complaints. This seemed to them one of those odd questions psychologists are prone to ask (often for no apparent reason). But they said that, indeed, one of his more noticeable characteristics was his loud and constant burping and talking about "pains" in his stomach. A gastrointestinal workup had been essentially negative; so the behavior in question was taken as part of his "psychosis."

I referred him for a neurological assessment, and the EEG

(electroencephalogram) report confirmed my suspicion of Temporal Lobe Epilepsy (TLE).* Norman Geschwind has reported that this type of seizure disorder is relatively rare in the general public but not among institutionalized persons. Because the symptoms of TLE are "behavioral," these can be misinterpreted as symptomatic of a psychiatric or behavioral disorder rather than the neurological one it is. There is one important difference between being labelled "assaultive" or "schizophrenic" and being diagnosed as having temporal lobe epilepsy: the differential diagnosis leads to a difference in treatment. If persons with TLE were treated the same as persons with schizophrenia, then there would be little point in determining which a person had. But the treatment (usually medication) for temporal lobe epilepsy can lead to its being resolved. There are no medical treatments, per se, for "assaultiveness," though everything from drugs to psychosurgery has been tried.

Neither temporal lobe epilepsy nor schizophrenia can be "cured." In both cases, one is essentially managing symptoms. But the symptoms of a seizure disorder are not managed with the drugs used to help with the symptoms of schizophrenia. Thus, to get the proper intervention, it is essential to make an accurate diagnosis.

I suppose there is no time when differential diagnosis is not important. In the emergency room, it can be a matter of life and death. But in the psychologist's testing room, it can make the difference between merely labelling a person and pursuing an effective approach. As a result, I try to work closely with neuropsychologists, neurologists, and other health care workers in diagnosing a disorder and formulating a program of treatment.

> Tina lived in the locked "dormitory" of a state training "school."
> She had been labelled "profoundly retarded." Those who worked
> with her initially found her to be a likable person. Her friendly
> attitude encouraged others to look forward to being with her. But
> Tina would—unpredictably—strike out. This would happen

---

*I suspected a physiological basis to his behavior because of the stereotypical pattern of hitting that he used (that is, always his left hand and always in the same way, regardless of the situation). I further suspected TLE because persons who have it often complain of upper gastrointestinal distress. This is an intuitively unlikely symptom constellation; nonetheless, it is useful to know.

quickly and with no warning. A person sitting to the right of her might suddenly be slapped hard across the face with the back of her right hand.

Retardation always has a physical basis in the central nervous system. This physical impairment is what leads to the difficulties a person labelled retarded might have with learning or in motor control. Neurology has made great strides in its understanding of the brain's workings, but at present our assessment of neurological functioning is nowhere as sophisticated as, for example, our abilities to assess cardiac functioning. Furthermore, many of the tests we use to assess intellectual and neurological functioning have been developed for a more general population. These tests have poor ability to discriminate among the different types of severe neurological damage that persons labelled retarded often have. Finally, persons labelled retarded often have difficulties in getting good medical services, although fortunately this seems to be growing less common. Many physicians and health professionals are uncomfortable working with persons with special needs. One mask for their lack of experience is the attitude, "Why bother? What difference will it make anyway?" One nonverbal man who had been labelled retarded appeared to be having trouble with his eyes; so he got an appointment with an ophthalmologist who did the examination as this man sat across the room from the doctor.

When a person seems to be responding to something not obviously present, the first thing to do is to have a complete physical examination with at least an EEG as a preliminary first step to ruling out a physical disorder. If a person becomes agitated about something that has happened and throws a cup, then we can see a certain cause and effect. But there are persons who for no *apparent* reason can become assaultive and apparently out of control. When these episodes show the same behaviors regardless of the situation, we should especially consider a physiological disorder.

For example, Tina's slapping seemed to be without any reason at all. There were various interpretations of her assaultiveness, though. Some persons found they had been hit when talking to someone else; so they felt that Tina was doing this for "attention." Others felt that she had been angered about something earlier and that her anger was only recently coming out in socially inappropriate ways. Sometimes, they noted, she would slap a wall instead of a person. Tina's response to these episodes, though, was to appear confused and upset at what had happened. This was interpreted as her having a "guilty conscience" and a fear of "consequences."

The clue that makes this seem like a neurological rather than a social issue is the consistency with which she acts. A person who gets angry is capable of doing many things to show this. Tina always displayed "anger" with the back of her right hand. Similarly, if she were delaying her expression of anger from an earlier event, she might show her irritation in more subtle or varied ways. In any case, the stereotypical hand movement and the confusion seemed to suggest a temporal lobe disorder which was in fact confirmed by an EEG. Incidentally, EEG is not a highly reliable instrument for this diagnosis. It is estimated that about 50 percent of the persons who have temporal lobe epilepsy do not show this on an EEG. As a result, when the EEG report is positive, then we are fairly confident that a neurological condition exists. If it is negative, then we can only say we do not know for certain.

Of course, not every unpleasant or puzzling behavior is dictated neurologically. It is important to make certain that the behavior we are challenged by is not persons' adaptation to a social environment they do not yet understand. When we find ways in which a behavior helps people, at least helps from their perspective, we have a different route to travel. But when we feel we have exhausted the social possibilities, we should pursue the neurological ones. It is important to rule out the physical and treatable possibilities for people's seemingly irrational behavior before we label them or blame them or try to treat their behavior as if it were their own choice.

Summary

There are some simple and basic steps that can help make the use of medications effective:

A referral for chemotherapy should be sufficiently specific so that a person unfamiliar with the behaviors involved could recognize them from the description provided. The frequency of the behavior should be noted as well as any pertinent circumstances in which it occurs.

Any medication should be administered with well-defined target behaviors listed and regularly reviewed. There should be a reasonable definition of what would constitute "success" for the medication as well as when such results could be expected. If a medication that should be effective within 72 hours has produced no change after a week, it should be discontinued. If it has been effective, how long should the person be maintained on this before being given a "drug holiday"?

The *Physician's Desk Reference* and a medical dictionary are helpful in getting accurate information about the possible side effects a given drug might induce.

Data and information should be done in the same way the baseline information was so that changes that correlate with the medication or various dosages of medication can be seen more clearly.

After the target behaviors have improved or been eliminated, then the drug should be removed to see if the behavior still exists. Drug holidays should be regularly scheduled to make certain that the original behavior the drug was intended for is controlled by the medication and by the medication only.

The use of medication, just like any other approach, must always be the best form of assistance we can offer rather than simply being the easiest.

— 6 —

Afterword

The approaches presented in this book are sometimes easy to misunderstand. Some have thought of them as "reverse psychology," as a way of tricking others into agreement by pretending to give them what they want. Deceit, of course, can be quite effective, especially in the short run. But on both a long- and short-term basis deceit is exactly opposite to the spirit in which all of this was developed. My interest is to find ways of working honestly and respectfully with others to develop trusting relationships. Slyly outwitting them is a poor starting point.

Ignorance can be the mother of wisdom; cleverness never. My own ignorance in working with persons I do not understand has taught me a great deal about how to live. Many of the things that others do confuse me. But that confusion is an opportunity to learn something and not to impose my sense of order. For example, when Karen meets a new person she shakes hands. The problem is that she will not let go. The ordinary impulse is to try to get away, which then makes holding a person's hand even more important for her because she never gets to do it on her own terms. Rather than wrestling ourselves free, we could say, "If you want to hold my hand, then let's sit a while and do it." If Karen cannot tell me why she needs to do this, then I can at least make some preliminary guesses. Instead of saying, "She does that to be manipulative," we might just as well guess, "She does that because she needs to establish that you really are a friend who will sit a few minutes with her." Instead of saying, "She's only doing

that for attention," we can just as easily say, "She really appreci-
ates knowing that people will spend time with her."

There will be times, though, when we really are busy and cannot spend five minutes holding hands with Karen. Perhaps as we
are sitting there with her, someone falls and needs some help up.
If we have been able to establish enough of a relationship with Karen, she will understand that we are saying no because of some
pressing outside reason and not because we do not like her or care
about her. But instead of saying, "Karen, I've got to help Bill, I'll
be back in a minute," we sometimes have the attitude of "setting
limits" or saying, "You just can't expect people to sit holding your
hand all day; get back to work."

If these approaches can be summarized quickly, they could be
thought of as respecting the needs and opinions of others regardless of what labels they might happen to have. This does not mean,
of course, that in respecting the wishes of others we necessarily
can grant them. If, on a rainy day, someone says, "I wish we could
have a picnic at the beach," we can reply—quite respectfully—"It
would be fun; too bad it's raining." But sometimes we do not share
the wish; we just say no to it. There are ways of saying no that en-
hance our relationships; there are also ways that tear them down.

My experience with all this has been mixed. Some persons find
this way of working a way to become the friendly helpers they had
wanted to be. Some persons say this is an ideal way of working,
but it just is not "realistic." The typical criticism I have been given
is that this approach is "naive," that the persons we work with
need "structure," "limits," "to learn consequences," and so on as
if somehow the approaches discussed here promoted anarchy and
unreality.

What I am advocating is that we give our friends the same opportunities to learn and use socially appropriate behavior as anyone else. This opportunity teaches the same natural "structure,"
"limits," and "consequences" that most of us learn and work with
in ordinary life. I think it is just as disrespectful to make rigid demands of the persons we work with as it is to say that they have
"suffered enough" and should never be expected to be more than
they please. Setting rigid limits is not much different from having
no expectations for growth; both provide uncaring ways of not
working with others or taking them seriously.

For example, when Kerry gets upset with something at work,
she goes into the supervisors' office and reads their magazines.
One common reaction to this is to tell Kerry that she should get
back to work. If she does not she can be given one more reminder

and then be physically "escorted" back to work. The rationale behind this is that Kerry needs to learn to respect the limits and property of others. Kerry has lived almost all her life in a state "training school" where she had no property of her own. She had a bed to sleep in, but that could be changed without notice. She might have a toothbrush, but it was kept locked in a cabinet. At no point in her life had she ever had a chance to learn what having something of her own was. Her life had taught her that you owned what you could grab or hang on to. Not surprisingly, Kerry had some issues about hoarding magazines or other things that struck her as worth keeping. With this kind of experience, it is not unusual that the idea of property that belonged to some persons and not to others was alien. That she could have her own magazines just as others could have theirs was a concept she had never actually experienced.

Kerry could be emphatic about staying in the office. When the persons working with her tried to move her physically out of it, she would hit them. Then they would try to time her out (since being timed out was the consequence of hitting). The question I have is whether it is worth fighting—literally—over the concept of private property with a person who has not yet learned what private property is. Is it not more to the point to teach her that she can get her own magazines, that she can have her own work area, and that those things will be respected and to teach her by modeling what it is we are talking about? Not only is it more helpful for Kerry; it is much more easily accomplished.

Since the socially unusual environment we have provided her—in this case, an institution—has taught Kerry socially unusual behavior, we can be confident that Kerry learns from her environment. As a result, we can shape her environment so that Kerry can learn success rather than failure. Changing a person's environment can be accomplished much more easily and more quickly than trying to shape her behavior.

If we have a magazine that is important to us, we can leave it at home or secure it, so when Kerry comes into the office, only magazines we are willing to part with are available to her. We could provide magazines for her in an area that does not interrupt others so she does not find them only in an inconvenient area. If she takes her magazine but sits and refuses to go back to work, we can say, "If you insist on sitting here, it must be something you need to do. But if you want to talk with me, I'll meet you back in the work area, and we can talk for a few minutes before you get back to work." This way, regardless of what Kerry chooses, she is cooperating with us as much as we are with her. She may want to test our willingness to provide for her by staying in the office for several hours. But she is unlikely to want to stay there for days on end. When she finally does return to work, she will be more confident that the persons she works with are more interested in cooperating with her than in controlling her.

Until Kerry has learned that everyone can get and keep possessions, we need patience in teaching her. Often we act as if the most important thing we had to teach is work skills. My experience has been that most of the persons we work for have far better vocational than social skills. If Kerry insists on sitting in an office when she is scheduled to be working, then we can take advantage of that moment to show her ways of cooperating in a social way. We can be flexible enough to realize that we cannot teach everything at once and that in moments like this Kerry can learn important social lessons. In doing this, we would not jeopardize her vocational abilities. In fact, we will be enhancing them, since persons who can do their work cooperatively are better employees than those with the same vocational skills but fewer social skills.

We can better meet a person's social and vocational needs with patient demonstration of how we can work cooperatively than with an abrupt display of irritation and an enforcing of "the rules." One common observation of persons who are labelled retarded is that they are rigid and need an unchanging routine in order to function. But when we show how inflexible we can be by insisting on addressing only work skills in a training program, we show how the same brush paints our portraits.*

Another misconception is that this approach is an effort to be "nice," to make no demands on persons with any sort of disability, to form a club in which we collaborate to keep such persons dependent on us but in a cozy environment safe from coldhearted scientists. As I have said, I think behavioral research has presented us with some of the few things we can feel confident about in the

---

*One group home supervisor explained to me the challenge of getting Sue to be more flexible. "She's so rigid as many retarded people are. When she comes home, she has to make her sandwich before taking her shower. I've tried to explain to her that's not how we do it. We shower first, then make our sandwiches. I've tried telling her that the food will still be there for her when she's done showering, but she won't listen." This struggle had gone on for some time until I pointed out that by the same logic the shower would still be there after she had made her sandwiches and was it possible that Sue was not the only person in this system being "rigid"?

social sciences. To devalue that seems impertinent and, finally, ig-
norant. Instead of ignoring these findings, I think it important to
introduce them to socially ordinarly environments. This is crucial
for a population that has been segregated from those environments.

The one attitude that disturbs me most, though, is the idea
that we must choose between being "nice" and being "therapeutic." Rather than being mutually exclusive, I think they are mutually inclusive. It is hard to do therapy without trust and some
mutual regard, and I think it is hard to have a friendly and supportive relationship with another person that is not in some way
"good" for the parties involved.

This book will have been a disappointment for the person who
is patient enough to read it through looking for effective or efficient
"techniques." Frankly, much of what has been shown is much less
efficient than more traditionally behavioral approaches if we meas-
ure outcome in strictly behavioral terms. These approaches often
seem, at least to me, to take longer. The difference, though, is not
in the conclusions we arrive at, but rather in the process of arriving there. Using food, tokens, verbal praise, or any of the other
traditional reinforcers, we can teach many skills to many persons.
But what is not taught in this approach is a social context. This is
why the approaches I have advocated take longer and are less clinically neat: they replicate ordinary relationships.

* * *

All professions work for their own undoing. Good teachers
hope their students will go beyond what they have to teach. Physicians work for their patients to be healthy. Those of us who work
for persons labelled retarded work for the day when our assistance
is no longer necessary. Sometimes that is hard for us to see. We
have been so used to thinking of persons with this label as unchanging or only slightly changeable. I suppose the reason for this
is that this label is based on irreversible organic deficit. But just
because a condition will never heal, it does not mean that a person cannot grow. There are persons who cannot see and are not
likely to, but do we really imagine them forever locked in a world
of dependence and helplessness? Persons with sensory or motor
challenges often use others to help them rise to those challenges
and learn to live as independently as they wish. There was a time
when a person who could not see or hear or walk was an object of
pity, but those days are passing. The day when persons labelled

retarded are seen as needing assistance and not maintenance, as needing our fellowship and not our pity, is just arriving.

It would be satisfying to see the persons we now label retarded not to be set apart because of their needs but rather to be respected as persons whose needs are met simply and naturally. One ideal would be for persons now labelled retarded to be thought of as simply another group in society—like persons who are left-handed. Left-handed persons often have to make adjustments in their daily lives, such as sitting at a different place at the table to eat comfortably, but nobody thinks the worse of them for it.

I would like to see this book become quaint and dated. But if the approaches suggested in this book were put into common usage, what would really change? The most important thing, for me, would be that we would no longer segregate either physically or socially the persons we work with.

The idea of normalization has helped us to reexamine the role of the institution, but this seems (so far) to have resulted in the compromise institution of group homes. This answers more directly the problem of physical segregation, but it still results in social segregation. Many persons living in group homes are not allowed out of them without supervision. But how many group homes have the resources for individual trips into the neighborhood? When a person living in such a house does travel with only one other person, it is sufficiently rare as to be called "a one-to-one community experience." My experience has been that even though there may be only eight persons living in a large house, those eight persons travel most often as a unit with one or two others who work with them. A group of nine or ten persons traveling together is labelling in and of itself. As a psychologist, I have given a certain amount of respect by society, and I have found psychologists as a group not much different to be with than any other random group of persons. But I would still be uncomfortable if most of my experience in society were in the constant company of seven other psychologists.

Our segregation of others, though, is more pervasive than simple things such as the emphasis on group activities. How many of us would be happy if we did not have sustaining and significant relationships? I suspect that one basic source of contentment for all of us to know that there is at least one person in our lives who needs us and whom we need. (This may also be a basic source of day-to-day irritation, but fighting requires a certain degree of intimacy.) For far too long, we have assumed that persons labelled retarded—especially those with the labels of profoundly retarded

or autistic—cannot form relationships or do not really need relationships. This sets up a cycle of self-fulfilling prophecies: if some
persons do not need to have relationships, we do not provide the
sort of life that would allow them, and since these persons have
never had relationships of any duration, they never learn to form
them. When we try to form relationships with them and they fail
to grasp what we are doing, we "prove" again that such persons
are incapable of doing this.

This genuinely shocks me. When I look at our culture in
general, at my friends in general, and my own life in particular, I
see how often making friends is a skill that requires practice and
experience. As relationships become more intimate, the ways they
work (or fail) are less obvious. Even casual working acquaintances
require us to be able to negotiate in order for the parties involved
to feel a sense of cooperation. It is only in folktales and popular
dramas where fantasies are played out that the purehearted can
overcome the truly evil to settle down to a life of happiness ever
after. In ordinary life we are all mixes of strong and weak, wise and
foolish, generous and mean, and our relationships with one another play off on those potentials in ways that are rarely all good
or all bad. My own life has been rich in the opportunities and the
necessities to learn how to get along with and to love others. And
in spite of the many blunders I have made in this, this is obviously
an aspect of life I would not lightly part with. Is your own life any
different? And yet how many of our friends who have been labelled
retarded can say another person needs them? And how many
know they are needed in an important way?

The chief barrier has been that we—as professionals—still see
persons labelled retarded as "clients" and not as our brothers and
sisters. I was talking to a group of persons about Larry, a teenager
who was just beginning to see himself as a man rather than as a
"cute little retarded boy." Developmentally, he was going through
the learning experience we associate with adolescence. Like most
of us at that point in our social lives, he was having crushes on his
teachers at school, on TV personalities, and some of the persons
who worked in his group home. He asked Paula, who worked there
on weekends, if he could be her boyfriend. She said, "No, Larry.
I'm staff and you're a client." I asked her what she would have said
if Peter, a man who also worked at the group home, had asked her
for a date. "I would have told him I already have a steady
boyfriend."

Sometimes this failure to take the importance of relationships
into account is used against our friends. "Elaine has been a prob-

lem. She prefers staff to her peers, and it's hard to get her to see she is just like the other five people she lives with here." Often, Elaine's behavior will be explained as "attention seeking." But as I have explained, a person seeks out attention not because attention is a goal, but because it is a tool: in this case Elaine might well be trying to get the attention of others as a way of beginning relationships with them. The persons she lives with might not have the skills to form relationships the way the persons who work in her house do. Typically, the response is not to teach Elaine how to make friends with anyone, regardless of that person's job or status, but to redirect her (for example, "When Elaine tries to monopolize staff, she should be redirected to another activity such as coloring or socializing with a peer"). In other words, "Don't try to use us as models for behavior. Look to your housemates. And when you have learned to have relationships, we will have one with you."

I suspect that some of the things we do for "behavior management" make sense to us because we do not have a relationship with the persons we work with. If we did, much of our "therapy" and "programming" would have a different form. But because we do not see the persons we work with as having a relationship with the world in most of the same ways that we do, we act with, for, and on them in ways that promote their being different from us rather then becoming more like us.

Recently I had a meeting with a group of persons providing direct service. This group and I had been working together for some time, and we had a friendly working relationship. By friendly, I mean that we respected one another, laughed at each others' jokes, and disagreed freely. But on this day, ours was the last meeting of a day in which I had felt discouraged and tired. They, in their turn, had been feeling stressed by the challenges of one woman who was hitting some of her co-workers. The conversation drifted into using "time out" for her. I had made it clear many times that I felt time out was an inappropriate consideration for persons they were trying to help. When they proposed it yet again, though, I lost patience. I told them that if they wanted to talk about this I would leave and they could continue without me. Someone pointed out that I was trying to use time out with them and it was not fair. Amused by this irony, we moved on to respond to this situation with a more respectful approach.

On the way out, though, I asked if my occasional impatience was something they found unnecessarily burdensome. One of the instructors just laughed and said, "Not really. We figure you go home and realize how carried away you get and that you remember how much you really do like us and how much we like you and it all works out." I thought that a sweet way to sum it up. But why do we so often expect the persons we work with to be less generous with us? And do we really want to be any less considerate of them?

References

American Psychiatric Association. *Diagnostic and statistical manual of mental disorders* (3rd ed.). Washington, D.C.: APA, 1980.

Ayllon, T. Intensive treatment of psychotic behavior by stimulus satiation and food reinforcement. *Behavior Research and Therapy*, 1963, *1*, 53–61.

Ayllon, T., & Michael, J. The psychiatric nurse as a behavioral engineer. *Journal of the Experimental Analysis of Behavior*, 1959, *2*, 323–334.

Azrin, N., & Foxx, R. *Toilet training in less than a day*. New York: Simon and Schuster, 1974.

Baumeister, A., & Klosowski, R. An attempt to group toilet train severely retarded patients. *Mental Retardation*, 1965, *2*, 323–334.

Carroll, S. W., Sloop, E. W., Mutter, S., & Prince, P. L. The elimination of chronic clothes ripping in retarded people through a combination of procedures. *Mental Retardation*, 1978, *16* (3), 246–249.

Dashiell, J. F. A quantitative demonstration of animal drive. *Journal of Comparative Psychology*, 1925, *5*, 205–208.

Dinkmeyer, D., & McKay, G. *Systematic training for effective parenting (parent's handbook)*. Circle Pines, Minn.: American Guidance Service, 1976.

Foxx, R. M. The use of overcorrection to eliminate the public disrobing (stripping) of retarded women. *Behavior Research and Therapy*, 1976, *14*, 53–61.

Foxx, R. M., & Azrin, N. Restitution: A method of eliminating aggressive-disruptive behavior of retarded and brain-damaged patients. *Behavior Research and Therapy*, 1972, *10*, 15–27.

Foxx, R. M., & Azrin, N. The elimination of autistic, self-stimulatory behavior by overcorrection. *Journal of Applied Behavior Analysis*, 1973a, *6*, 1–14.

Foxx, R. M., & Azrin, N. *Toilet training the retarded: A rapid program for day and nighttime independent toileting.* Champaign, Ill.: Research Press, 1973b.

Foxx, R. M., & Azrin, N. Dry pants: A rapid method of toilet training children. *Behavior Research and Therapy,* 1973c, *11,* 435–442.

Foxx, R. M., & Martin, E. D. Treatment of scavenging behavior (coprophagy and pica) by overcorrection. *Behavior Research and Therapy,* 1975, *13,* 153–162.

Freud, S. *An outline of psycho-analysis* (translated by J. Strachey). New York: Norton, 1949.

Gessell, A, & Ilg, F. L. *Infant and child in the culture of today.* New York: Harper, 1943.

Gold, M. W. *Try Another Way Training Manual.* Champaign, Ill: Research Press, 1980.

Groos, K. *The play of man* (translated by E. L. Baldwin). New York: Appleton, 1901.

Hamilton, J., Stephens, L., & Allen, P. Controlling aggressive and destructive behavior in severely retarded institutionalized residents. *American Journal of Mental Deficiency,* 1967, *71,* 852–856.

Hebb, D. O. *The organization of behavior.* New York: Wiley, 1949.

Hebb, D. O., & Thompson, W. R. The social significance of animal studies. In G. Lindzey (ed.), *Handbook of social psychology. Vol. I.* Cambridge, Mass.: Addison-Wesley, 1954, pp. 532–561.

Krech, D., Crutchfield, R. S., Livson, N, and Wilson, W. A. *Elements of Psychology.* New York: Knopf, 1974.

Laski, H. J. "The Dangers of Disobedience," *Harper's,* 1929, vol. 159, pp. 1–10 (quoted in Krech, D., Crutchfield, R.S., Livson, N., & Wilson, W. A. *Elements of psychology.* New York: Knopf, 1974).

Levy, D. M. Oppositional syndromes and oppositional behavior. In D. H. Hoch & J. Zubin (eds.), *Psychopathology of childhood.* New York: Grune and Stratton, 1955, pp. 204–226.

Milgram, S. Group pressure and action against a person. *Journal of Abnormal Social Psychology,* 1964, *69,* 137–143.

Nissen, H. W. A study of exploratory behavior in the white rat by means of the obstruction method. *Journal of Genetic Psychology,* 1930, *37,* 361–376.

Nye, R. D. *Three psychologies: Perspectives from Freud, Skinner and Rogers.* Monterey, Calif.: Brooks/Cole, 1981.

Paul, H., & Miller, J. Reduction of extreme deviant behaviors in a severely retarded girl. *Training School Bulletin,* 1971, *67*(4), 193–197.

Schaefer, H., & Martin, P. *Behavioral Therapy.* New York: McGraw-Hill, 1969.

Skinner, B. F. *Science and human behavior.* New York: Macmillan, 1953.

Skinner, B. F. Origins of a behaviorist. *Psychology Today,* 1983, *17* (9), 22–33.

Thompson, T. & Grabowski, J. *Behavior modification and the mentally retarded.* New York: Oxford University Press, 1972.

Vukelich, R., & Hake, D. Reduction of dangerously aggressive behavior in a severely retarded resident through a combination of positive reinforcement procedures. *Journal of Applied Behavior Analysis*, 1971, *4*, 215–225.

White, R. Motivation reconsidered: The concept of competence. *Psychological Review*, 1959, *66*, 297–333.

White, R. Competence and the psychosexual stages of development. In M. R. Jones (ed.), *Nebraska Symposium on Motivation*. Lincoln: University of Nebraska Press, 1960, pp. 97–141.

Woolfolk, R. L., & Richardson, F. C. Behavior therapy and the ideology of modernity. *American Psychologist*, 1984, *39* (7), 777–786.

Author Index

Subject Index

About the Author

Herbert Lovett was educated at Bowdoin College, Yale, Harvard, and University of Rhode Island. In addition to working directly as a therapist with persons with special needs, Dr. Lovett has consulted with many residential, vocational, and training programs.